I've known Gina for fifteen years. I admired her tenacity as she dealt with an autistic son. I watched her exhaust every avenue possible, and with God's blessing Ethan has become her miracle child. Now as I'm starting this journey with my two-year-old nephew, her mentoring and special needs resources have been a comfort to me in this unknown territory. I'm grateful she has put this amazing journey in print to help others as well. Be blessed!

JODY BRASSFIELD
respite care worker

In the early days of our daughter's diagnosis with autism, we were just as lost as she was. We did not know what to do, or where to start, until we met the Walden family. Then it looked like there might actually be a light at the end of the tunnel. They gave us the hope and the support that we desperately needed. They shared their hard experience with us, showed us how to deal with the school district, and how to set up the IEP meeting. Watching Ethan grow up and defeat autism has given us a lot of hope.

MOE AND MOJGAN AHMADI
parents of a daughter with autism

As a teacher, working with special needs children can be a struggle. I have also talked with many parents who feel helpless and do not know where to turn for help. I have shared the Walden's story and the tools that they have used with many of my friends, colleagues, and parents. Now I am very happy to be able to share this book with them, so they can believe for their very own, *Brand New Day*.

HILARY MARTINO
kindergarten teacher

After speaking with Gina and meeting Ethan, a renewed hope was birthed in me. God used her to speak hope into a hopeless diagnosis for my son. Every time I have my "low" days with Jaden and I start to feel discouraged, the Lord always brings back to remembrance, Ethan. To me, *A Brand New Day* is like Gina having a personal conversation about Ethan's story with every single family affected by autism to the global community. *A Brand New Day* is the beacon of light that is so desperately needed for those living in the world of autism. It breathes life and encouragement, not from an autism professional's standpoint, but from a personal perspective where one can feel the blood, sweat, and tears of a family battling autism.

JOHN AND LEOLA ALLMOND
parents of son a with autism

Gina and Brian have helped my family stand up and advocate for our son. They gave us hope and showed us to stand strong for our family. I must say their faith and guidance have made a huge difference, not only in our son's life, but our whole family.

PETER AND LAURA QUINTANA
parents of a son with autism

Some of us are fighting for our children, some for ourselves, our marriages, our health, and our freedoms. Whatever your story and situation in life is, *A Brand New Day* will be an inspiration, and like a cold drink of water to a weary and thirsty soldier, it will refresh you as you begin your own brand new day.

SCOTT AND RACHEL CENTER
parents of a son with autistic-like behaviors

a brand

New Day

a brand New Day

faith, music,
and victory
over autism

BRIAN & GINA WALDEN

TATE PUBLISHING
AND ENTERPRISES, LLC

Scriptures taken from the *Holy Bible, New International Version*®, NIV®. Copyright © 1973, 1978, 1984 by Biblica, Inc.™ Used by permission of Zondervan. All rights reserved worldwide. www.zondervan.com

The opinions expressed by the author are not necessarily those of Tate Publishing, LLC.

This book is designed to provide accurate and authoritative information with regard to the subject matter covered. This information is given with the understanding that neither the author nor Tate Publishing, LLC is engaged in rendering legal, professional advice. Since the details of your situation are fact dependent, you should additionally seek the services of a competent professional.

Published by Tate Publishing & Enterprises, LLC
127 E. Trade Center Terrace | Mustang, Oklahoma 73064 USA
1.888.361.9473 | www.tatepublishing.com

Tate Publishing is committed to excellence in the publishing industry. The company reflects the philosophy established by the founders, based on Psalm 68:11,
"The Lord gave the word and great was the company of those who published it."

Book design copyright © 2012 by Tate Publishing, LLC. All rights reserved.
Cover design by Kristen Verser
Interior design by April Marciszewski
Photography by Michael Rivera

Published in the United States of America

ISBN: 978-1-61862-618-9
1. Family & Relationships / Autism Spectrum Disorders
2. Biography & Autobiography / Personal Memoirs
12.03.15

DEDICATION

To Ethan Scott Walden and all of Ethan's Angels

We dedicate this book to our son Ethan. Although many have been affected by the trials of autism, it is Ethan that has overcome. This is his testimony, one of God's goodness to remember and speak of forever.

We cannot forget the fact that we could not have made it through these times without the help of so many wonderful people that God placed in our lives. We like to refer to them as Ethan's Angels. Each has been a special part in our life as we have walked down the path that led to

Ethan's healing. We would like to take this opportunity to thank:

Devin Walden, Frank Foglio, Rich & Kim Walden, Julia Foglio, Jim & Nancy Walden, Travis & Brandy Henson, Heather Crudo, Ame Vigil, Janelle Bruner, Tiffany & Angelina Lewis, Patty Galardo, Reanna Bullard, Tracy Otamo, Kelli Wilms, Candice Lambert, Toni Cervantes, Paula DiCosola, Gracie Vandepoppe, Andrea Salazar, Brad McDuffee, Julie Tolerico, Tracy & Elizabeth

Garrison, Zondelyn Noble, Marianne Kyle, Christina Leroy, Allison Summers, Avril Amarais, Karen Connell, Mary Garrison, Melissa Rivera, Michael & Tammy Rivera, MIP Photos, Ann Marie Ayala, Armondo and Jackie Flores, Mistee Rios, Stephanie Castro, Dr. Thomas Lin, Tina and Annie Westrick, JJ Johnston, Cameron & Julie Ruffin, Steve & Veronica Mendoza, Pastors Mike & Sue Bryan, David & Dionne Archibeck, Dan & Jessica Roth, and last but not least, Pastors Jim & Deborah Cobrae.

A special thanks to Dr. Dennis Sempebwa of Eagles Wings International for his friendship, support, and collaborative development of this story.

Table of Contents

WALDEN FAMILY

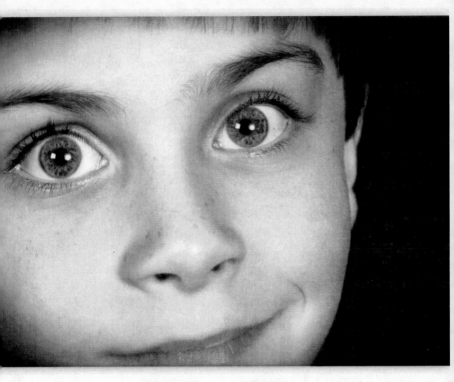

Season One

A BRAND NEW DAY

It was 7 o'clock in the morning when I walked into the boys' room to wake them up for school. I reached down and touched Ethan's back and said, "Good morning, Ethan. Are you ready for a brand new day?"

He rolled over, opened his big blue eyes, and looked up at me. It was not just his mouth that smiled, I could see the smile in his eyes; his whole face gleamed with excitement. He reached up and gave me a big hug, jumped down from his bed and ran down the hall. He couldn't wait to start this new day; today was his fifth birthday.

Five o'clock that afternoon I stood in amazement as all of his friends came in to celebrate my child, who according to his doctor, may never be able to make friends. I watched as Ethan took his best friend by her hand, and with joy and excitement ran from one bouncer to the next, laughing, jumping, and playing as if he never had this terrible disorder called autism.

I followed him and his friends, videotaping their every move. Although I did my best to record the whole thing, I couldn't seem to hold the camera still as I watched the promises of God play out in front of me. Only a few of my closest friends could see the emotions of the past three years streaming down my face in the form of tears. It was exactly as God said it would be. Ethan was healed; he was a new child. He was interacting, playing, and laughing like every other five-year-old in the room.

I don't think the other parents would believe what we had been through. No one there knew the road we had to walk, the fights we fought, or the prayers we cried for our son. Only God knew the whole story. He knew every step He ordered, every door He opened, and every path He made to lead us to where we are today.

I've always known that God is faithful, and today He has indeed proven Himself faithful to me. This really is a brand new day: Wednesday, May 19, 2009, the day that my family and I declared victory over autism.

Season Two

I was just six years old standing in front of the congregation at the Christian Center in San Bernardino, California. As the music played, I looked into the crowd with excitement. I was about to sing my first song in front of a church full of people. I was wearing a baby blue dress with the cutest little ruffles. Next to me stood my grandfather who was wearing one of his many church suits. He reached down and put his hand on my shoulder as we walked forward to sing our first duet. Was I nervous? No. I was driven to sing from birth, and I wanted to share the gift of music that was within me.

Papa Boone, as I called him, loved to sing with me. In fact, he gave me my first singing lesson. Papa would come over to our house a couple times a week, so he and I could sing together. After months of working, Papa announced, "Gina, it's time to share our song with the church." I did not know at the time, but the song he taught me to sing was a confirmation of a word he heard from God. God had told Papa that I would one day sing to the nations. The promise was proven to me by our very first song, "I am a Promise."

For many years, I attended my papa's church. It was there that I learned about God, established a foundation of faith, and developed my gift of singing. Then at the age of ten I recorded my first album and like many young recording artists, my daddy was my manager. He believed in me and encouraged me to pursue my aspirations in music. Soon after, I was singing in many churches around the area. This was definitely what I wanted to do with my life; I loved to sing, I loved to tell others about God, and I loved to share music with other people.

My dad's parents were also in ministry. My grandfather, Frank Foglio, was one of the founding members of the Full Gospel Businessmen's Fellowship International. Papa Foglio, as I called him, was also a bestselling author. He had written a book entitled *Hey God*, which is a story about my great-grandmother's faith and the miracles she saw God perform in her large Italian family.

My grandparents stayed very busy holding meetings and conferences around the world, but when they were in town, they too gave me the opportunity to share my music at their meetings. Needless to say, I come from a long line of Christian ministers, and now I was taking the torch of ministry and starting my own legacy.

Over the next few years, I shared my music at churches, school chapels, conferences and outreaches. As times changed and music evolved, I stopped singing the hymns and ballads that I grew up on and started performing songs for the younger generation. As I recorded more upbeat Christian music, more opportunities continued to open for me.

One Friday night, I was booked to perform at a local dance club. It was Christian night, and I opened for five local rappers known as the *Private Boyz*. In between our sets and late into the night the guest DJ played Christian music as a hundred or so young adults danced and worshiped.

The next morning my father received a call from a man named Scott Blackwell, owner and producer of N'Soul Records. He told my dad that he was the DJ at the club last night and was interested in using me for a new idea he had for the Christian music industry. He explained that he had a vision to take popular praise and worship songs and remix them for the younger generation. He continued to say that he wanted me to be the featured vocalist for the project. The project would be called *Nitro Praise*.

As a senior in high school, at just seventeen years of age, I was signed to a music deal. My childhood dream of singing professionally had come true. My first worship song on the album was entitled, *More Precious than Silver*. It became a big radio hit. Not only did it reach the Christian billboard charts, it set a record by staying there forty weeks.

My boyfriend, Brian, was very supportive of my dream. He followed me to every concert, setting up my product table and running the sound system. We dated for about a year, and then on February 14, 1994, he asked me to marry him. Eleven months later, we stood in a beautiful church, in front of a few hundred of our closest friends and family as Papa Boone led us in our marriage vows. Although I was only nineteen years old, and Brian just twenty-one, we both knew that God was leading us into a life of ministry together.

I had become known as "The Voice of Nitro Praise," and over the next ten years, I helped record seven Nitro Praise projects in addition to three of my own CDs. My music and videos were heard in many nations around the world. And we were blessed to travel and perform for thousands of people. Most importantly, we saw many come forward and accept Jesus as their personal Lord and Savior. We witnessed many miracles and saw people set free from sickness, diseases, addictions, and unhealthy lifestyles. We saw others answer the call to lay down their weapons, take off their gang colors, and give up their destructive lifestyles.

I knew that I had been made for such a time as this, and I was having the time of my life serving God and using the gift of music that He had given me. I was encouraged over and over again by what I saw God do in the lives of His people and I was continually reminded that God could do anything.

Although I had seen the hand of God perform many miracles, I had never been in a place where I needed a miracle myself. I saw God bring healing to many children, but I never thought I would soon beg Him to heal one of mine.

I'M YOURS

Surely I was made for such a time as this
I'm in the moment I'm created for
Made for your pleasure,
    Your Glory, Your Delight
Lord you are my treasure You're my all

I will Bless you Lord with all my heart
I will Praise you with my voice
With all I am and all I long to be
Everything I am is Yours, I'm Yours

Merciful Savior, the strength of my life
I'm captured in the wonder of your ways
With Joy of my salvation, I cannot refrain
I will not keep silent I will praise

I will bless you Lord with all my heart
I will Praise you with my voice
With all I am and all I long to be
Everything I am is Yours, I'm Yours

Lord you are my portion,
    my exceeding great reward
Lord you are my refuge, you're
    my shelter in the storm
Purchased with your precious
    blood, I am not my own
I will not be silent I will praise

Season Three

While I was recording a music video in the summer of 1999, I felt in my heart that God was telling me the end of this season was coming. While taking a break between scenes, He showed me that I was going to enter a time of rest. He said, "I am going to sit you down for a season to teach you and develop you for your future."

I didn't like what I was hearing, but I knew in my heart that God was going to move me out of the public eye for a while. I responded by thinking "Why would I want to stop singing? I love to sing and minister in music." But as I sat against a shade tree taking a few minutes to myself something inside me knew that the end was near. I wondered what I would do next. Immediately, the thought of another childhood dream shot through my mind. I always wanted a family with two beautiful children. I dreamed of tickles and giggles and music filling our house. Later in the week as I shared my thoughts with Brian, we decided that this was the perfect time to start that family.

Over the next year, my music ministry slowed down, and my focus started to change as I thought about becoming a mommy.

Since we were not traveling as much as we used too, we found a church near our home and sat under the teaching of a great pastor. After a few months, I decided to volunteer my time to the music team. It was there that God was going to start to teach me some things about myself and true worship.

With more time at home, I was now establishing a new daily routine. Each morning as Brian left for work I would walk three houses down the street, sit in my mother's kitchen, and share conversation and a cup of coffee. My mother and I were best friends. We loved to go for walks, spend time shopping, go out to lunch, and run errands together. For many months, mom kept asking, "When are you going to give me a grandbaby?" When she asked, I tried to ignore her and brush it off. I didn't want to tell her that Brian and I were already working on it. I thought it would be more fun to wait and surprise her.

After four months of unsuccessful attempts, I finally received the news that I had been waiting for. I was pregnant. As Brian returned home from work that day, I met him in the driveway, greeting him with a kiss. I led him into our living room where he found a picnic set up on the floor. By the fireplace was a large baby blanket set up with our best china. Hanging in one corner was a banner that read, "Congratulations, it's a Boy," and in the other corner, "Congratulations, it's a Girl."

With excitement in his eyes, he looked at me and said, "Are we having twins?"

"I don't think so, I think I'd rather start with one."

"So this is really happening. We're going to have a baby?"

I was very happy to respond, "Yes, honey, we really did it. You're going to be a daddy."

As we sat and ate together, we talked about our hopes and dreams for our children. Would we have a boy or a girl? What would they grow up to be like? Would they look like me or be tall and handsome like their daddy? I could tell that Brian was excited when he said, "Maybe we will have twins, a boy and a girl. Wouldn't that be awesome?"

Later that night, Brian and I went out and bought a little brown bear that read, "I Love Grandma." I wrapped it in paper and put it in a gift bag so I could surprise my mom with the news.

The next day, I walked down the street for our usual morning coffee. As she poured me a cup, I placed the bag on her counter. "What's this?" she asked. "Oh, just open it, and you'll see." With one look my mom proceeded to jump around the kitchen, giggling with excitement

Later that week mom and I went shopping, she bought me maternity clothes, baby toys, and diapers; she even wanted to buy a stroller and some baby furniture. If I hadn't stopped her, I think she would have bought everything in the store.

Before long I had a list of appointments set up with my doctor. I bought some books on what to expect during pregnancy, labor, and delivery, and I was looking forward to the experience of carrying this creation for the next nine months.

Because the first couple months went by normally I assumed I would be healthy enough to sing through my pregnancy. So when I received a call asking me to sing at a 9-11 tribute concert, I gladly accepted.

On the day of the concert, I stood in my bathroom with three of my background singers as we did each other's hair and makeup. Suddenly, I bent over in pain. I wasn't sure what was going on until my pain was soon accompanied with bleeding. I tried to remain calm but anxiety quickly overcame me.

I called my doctor's office and asked to speak to the doctor, but the only one available was his nurse. She told me that spotting was common in some women and not to worry unless I start bleeding heavily. Everyone in the house tried to calm my nerves and reassure me, but nothing seemed to help.

At my insistence the nurse scheduled a checkup with the doctor first thing Monday morning. As I hung up the phone I not only wondered how I'd make it through the weekend, but also, how I was going to sing *God Bless America* that night. That was the first and only concert I ever had to cancel.

Monday morning the doctor examined me, poked around my stomach, and listened for a heartbeat. He did not say anything out of the ordinary or seem too concerned, but to be safe, he sent me down for an ultrasound. Deep inside, I knew something wasn't right. I was unsettled and worried; I had to make sure my baby was ok.

To my frustration, the X-ray department told me that there were no available appointments for the next two weeks. I wanted to scream. I couldn't wait two weeks to find out what was happening. I was going to go crazy if I had to wait to see what was going on inside of me.

One of the nurses could see that I was distraught and called me over to see if she could help. She introduced herself as Sara. I told her that I was pregnant with my first child and that my husband and I had been trying to start a family. She asked how long I had been married. "Six years," I said.

"Wow, have you been trying the whole time?" she asked. "No," I said, "only about four months."

She could see I was a nervous wreck, so she asked me to sit down and to let her see what she could do. As she disappeared into the back room, I sat down and waited for her return. I held my stomach and prayed, "Oh God, please let my baby be alright". A couple minutes later, Sara called my name and walked me right back to the ultrasound technician. She had worked a miracle for me and pulled some strings, so I did not have to wait any longer.

Although the technician could not disclose any information or read my ultrasound, she didn't need to; her face said it all. My worst fears were then confirmed by the doctor; I was having a miscarriage.

With my heart breaking, I went home and packed up all of the maternity clothes, the toys, and baby supplies that we had just bought and shut them into what would have been our baby's nursery. I tried to forget about the miscarriage and get on with life, but the pain of losing this baby would not leave me. One day while imagining who my baby would have been and what it would have looked like I decided to give it a name. In my heart I felt like I was going to have a girl so I named her Sara.

This was the first time in my life that I had experienced real pain. I did not know that your heart could really ache like mine did. I had given up my music ministry, and now I had lost my baby. I felt like my world was falling apart around me. I remember crying myself to sleep each night. The only thing that helped calm me down was the voice of my husband singing worship songs to God. Brian would lie next to me, hold my hand, and sing me to sleep. It was his response that helped teach me the importance of worshiping God, not just through the good times, but also through the storms of life.

I tried to cover my pain by staying busy and serving at church, but my emotions led me into a deep depression. Alone during the day, I found myself questioning God. "God, what are you doing with me? I thought you wanted me to stop singing and start a family? What is this all about? Are you really with me? Where did you go? I thought you said that you would never leave me nor forsake me."

Although I knew that God was with me, I felt all alone—maybe even betrayed. God had taken me away from that which I loved, singing to thousands across the nation, and had put me in a little church in the middle of the woods. He took me from the spotlight and placed me in a small congregation of people, most of whom didn't even know my name, and now I had lost my baby.

Maybe I did something wrong. Was God punishing me? As I sat there complaining, I was taken back to the word I heard from God a few months ago. He told me He was going to sit me down for a season and teach me some things. As those memories flooded my mind—as those words echoed deep inside my spirit, I whispered, "Forgive me, Lord, I have been looking at this all wrong. What do you want to teach me? Help me to see through this pain and trust you. I know that you have a plan and a purpose in all of this, and I pray that it would be fulfilled in me, in Jesus's name."

Next Sunday I went to church expecting to hear from God. As worship started I was ready to press through the issues of the past few weeks and get into God's presence. But something was still wrong. The worship team was off tune 'and, in my opinion, many of the vocalists needed voice lessons. I just couldn't seem to press through it all and get into God's presence. As I stood there trying to worship, I began to see how God was using their imperfections to teach me some things. He seemed to be saying, "Gina, it's not just about the quality of sound and the production of the show. I am more interested in the right position of the heart." God was taking this opportunity to shake me up and teach me about true worship.

After service I went up for prayer, and it was there that I did get a word from God. A guest speaker was there that day and prayed over me. As he prayed, he paused, and then said "God is going to hide you for a season, but there will be a day when you will be released to share your story with the world."

At home I contemplated those words and wondered what story I would tell. Did God want to use my miscarriage to somehow help other people? Could this hurt and pain that I am feeling be the story that I would share with the world? Over the next few days as I spent time with God, He continued to teach me, refine me, and bring me to a place of surrender.

I SURRENDER

In sweet adoration I stand before you now
In awe of you I come and humbly bow
I give to you my life,
    I'm lifting up my hands
I give to you the things I don't
    understand, I surrender

I surrender to you
I'm falling on my knees
I know you're all I need
I surrender at your feet
I'm weary but I know
Your touch restores my soul
I surrender at your throne, I surrender

Lord I surrender to you and you alone
I want to feel your grace come in this place
I meet you at your throne
I feel your presence so powerful
Now I give to you my heart
and all that I am, I surrender

Season Four

A year after the miscarriage, Brian and I decided that it was time to try again and start a family. We tried for months, each time ending in disappointment. There were a couple times that I thought I was pregnant, I even took a few tests. If I missed my period, even by a couple days, we would take a pregnancy test and wait in anticipation to see two blue lines. Frustrated, we finally stopped trying and decided to wait. As soon as we did, it happened. I was pregnant!

Deep inside, I feared losing this baby too. As a few months with no complications, my fears began to fade away. It was not until week twenty-eight that complications arose. A trip to the restroom revealed that I had started to spot. I cried out in prayer, "Oh no, Lord, not now. I can't lose this baby too. Please God!"

A trip to the doctor revealed that everything was fine. But to be safe, the doctor did restrict me to bed rest until the baby arrived.

At home sitting still, I had a lot of time to listen to God's voice and I learned to hear Him. He taught me how to be still and trust Him.

The last eight weeks of my pregnancy seemed to last forever, but they too did pass. Then early in the morning on July 2, 2002, we welcomed Devin James Walden into the world. He quickly became known as "Devin from heaven."

The dark season of life had turned to sunshine. Devin was truly a gift from God. He took to nursing right away and was easy to care for. He was a happy baby, quick to smile and respond to those around him. Since he hardly ever cried, we could take him to nice restaurants and to the movies without fear of him disrupting those around us.

My mom and dad were proud to be grandparents. We would now call them *Mimi* and *Papa*. Mimi and I continued our daily meetings for breakfast, but now we had a special guest to share our time with. She loved pushing him around in his stroller and showing him off to all of her neighbors, and she was glad to watch him if I needed to take a shower or run any errands. Devin from heaven was a blessing to all of us, and he was a very good baby. Years later when we had our second child, we realized just how easy he really was.

Season Five

ETHAN SCOTT WALDEN

Devin was about a year old when we started planning for our second child. We wanted our children to be about two years apart so they would grow up together, be best friends, and close enough in age to support each other through school and life.

We had left the little church in the mountains and where now attending a mega-church in San Bernardino. It was during the summer of 2003 that we started attending the Rock Church and World Outreach center. Out of all of the churches that we had visited over our years of ministry, there was something that set this church apart. They had some of the most anointed music, and to top it off, the pastor taught on relevant, real-life issues. We could see that this church had a heart to reach people for God and impact our city as well as the world.

Three months later, I became pregnant with our second son. This pregnancy went by without any complications. Then on May 19, 2004, at eight-fifteen in the morning, Ethan Scott Walden was born. He was beautiful, had big blue eyes, ten fingers and ten toes. Ethan looked a lot like his big brother, but although they looked alike there was something a little different about Ethan.

When Devin was a baby he laid still and always seemed happy. Ethan, on the other hand, was a crier, very wiggly, and easily agitated. Unlike Devin, Ethan was restless at night and would not sleep. We were fortunate if we got any sleep at all. Although we were somewhat surprised by their differences, we were not too shocked as friends had told us that the second child is almost always harder than the first.

We brought Ethan home from the hospital hoping to get him into a nightly routine of sleep, but he was having none of it. It seemed like this little child didn't need much sleep at all. Brian and I quickly learned to work in shifts and take turns with Ethan so we could both get a little sleep. We found that the only way we could get Ethan to sleep was to wrap him tight, hold him in an upright position and rock him to sleep. But as soon as we stopped rocking he would wake up screaming.

Devin had just turned two years old. Like every two-year-old, he needed our time, attention, love, and guidance, but Ethan demanded all that we had. With Brian back at work, tending to our two young children became overwhelming. I soon realized that having Mimi down the street wasn't just a blessing but a necessity. Mimi helped take care of Devin during the day, so I could spend time trying to figure out our little Ethan.

One of the biggest challenges was getting Ethan to eat. I had committed to breast-feed both of my children for at least a year, but feeding Ethan was more like a wrestling match than a mother/son bonding experience. I had to fight him just to get him to hold still long enough to nurse.

After every feeding, I would burp him and then lay him down on his baby blanket. Instead of lying peacefully, he would cry, toss his little body from side to side, and kick his legs in the air. I wondered if I was doing something wrong or maybe he had a bad case of gas. I knew that Devin did not have these problems when he ate, so I thought that maybe Ethan wasn't latching on correctly or maybe taking in too much air. I tried to hold him in every position, and I made sure to burp him after every meal. But nothing seemed to help. We even tried a liquid supplement that was supposed to help with gas and take away his agitation after eating.

After talking to Ethan's pediatrician, I was told that our hospital had a lactation consultant on site. After seeing her and being told that I was doing everything right, she said, "Some babies take longer to learn how to breastfeed than others. Don't worry, he seems to be healthy. Just give it some time, and he'll get it."

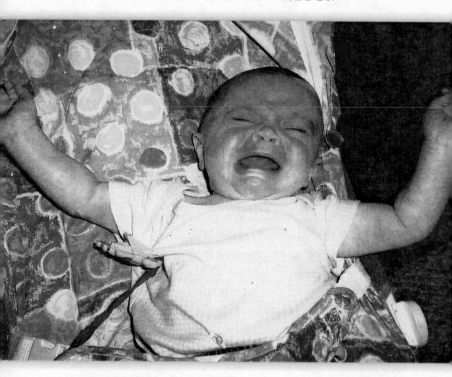

Though he looked normal, and the doctors said he was fine, deep inside, Brian and I knew that something wasn't right with our little man. In spite of our suspicions, we decided to learn how to appreciate Ethan for the way he was and accept his different personality. I guess everyone was right when they said our second child would be harder than our first.

On Ethan's first birthday, he took his first steps just like his brother had done before him, but we continued to see many other differences in their development. For instance, Ethan did not respond to anyone that came into the room. Even when they tried to get his attention, he acted as if he could not hear them. If someone tried to play with him, we could tell that he was uncomfortable and would rather play by himself. If he could talk, I think he would have asked us to leave him alone.

All the stress that came from trying to care for Ethan was almost too much for me to handle. Soon after, my mom started to have health problems. She started feeling very sick and became too weak to help with Devin so with both boys at home my days became very busy.

I remember one morning when Brian had just left for work. It was still dark outside, and the house was quiet and peaceful. I so wanted to stay in bed and get a little more sleep, because we had been up with Ethan most of the night. Even so, I decided to get up and enjoy a little quiet time or maybe take a shower. I walked across the house to make sure the boys were still sleeping. As I peeked into their rooms, I could see them sound asleep. They looked so sweet and innocent tucked in their beds.

I tiptoed back across the house, hoping they would sleep long enough for me to take a nice hot shower. I jumped in enjoying the shower like it was a tropical waterfall...

My peaceful escape suddenly ended as Devin came running in yelling, "Smoke! Smoke!"

I leaped out of the shower, almost slipping on the floor. I grabbed Devin and a towel as I took off running across the house. Approaching Ethan's room I saw that Devin was right. The air was full of white smoke. I noticed a white substance all over the floor, the furniture and all over Ethan. Devin then said, "Look mom I made smoke," as he pointed to the container of baby powder he emptied all over Ethan's room. "Looks like smoke huh?" He then ran into his room put on a fireman's hat and ran back toward me making siren sounds.

Standing in Ethan's doorway I didn't know if I should laugh or cry. I started to clean up the mess when I noticed I still had shampoo in my hair and only one leg shaved. I shook my head as I thought to myself, *I sure have come a long way from my days as a Christian recording artist.*

Ethan soon woke up and started his normal routine of fussing and whining. No matter what I did, he never seemed to be happy or satisfied. When I put him in his high chair to feed him breakfast, he stiffened his body so I couldn't strap him in. Once he was secure, I sat next to him and tried to feed him, but everything I put in his mouth he spit out and smeared all over himself. There were a few things I got in his mouth, but instead of swallowing he held the food in his cheeks. I rubbed his little face, trying to encourage him to swallow, and he bit my hand.

I could tell the only thing he wanted was his bottle of milk. Frustrated, I left him in his highchair drinking his bottle, and I went back to finish cleaning up Devin's smoke experiment.

A few minutes later, I heard a shaking noise coming from the other room. I hurried to see what was going on and noticed Devin quietly watching TV, but Ethan was missing. He had escaped from his highchair.

Turning into the kitchen, I saw that he'd emptied an entire box of cereal on the floor. I rushed toward him, yelling his name as he proceeded to pour a quart of milk all over it.

I was so frustrated, I grabbed the container of yogurt that I had been trying to feed him and threw it against the wall. I yelled at the top of my lungs to let the whole world know that I quit! I couldn't take anymore. Somebody else was going to have to take care of these kids. Even with all my yelling, Ethan never even turned around to look at me. Devin did look over but quickly returned to watching TV like nothing happened.

Pausing for a moment, I contemplated my actions. It was out of my character to raise my voice, let alone throw something. I realized then that getting angry and frustrated was not going to solve my problems. I was the grown up and throwing tantrums was not going to fix anything.

I called Brian at work and although he tried to be encouraging, he didn't have much to say. He did tell me to be patient and keep them on a schedule, but he really didn't help at all. I understood that he was busy and needed to stay focused on work. Since I stopped singing, his job was the only source of income, and with only one income, finances were more of a concern.

Once Brian did come home, I tried to tell him about my day, but he was busy shuffling through the mail, only half listening to me. He then came and gave me a big hug and said, "I'm sorry you had a rough day."

He started to walk away then paused, and with a smirk on his face, said, "Want to make love? That always makes me feel better." All I could do was laugh. It seemed like everyone wanted something from me, but I had no more to give.

Season Six

Devin had just turned three years old and was now old enough to start preschool. We had never planned on him starting at such an early age, but we thought it would help reduce the stress of my long days. It would also be beneficial to him and help him get ready for a structured school program.

We looked at numerous pre-k centers in our area but what we found was not exactly what we were looking for. Some friends of ours recommended we try a Christian School down in San Bernardino. Although we loved the school, Brian and I agreed that driving up and down the mountain twice a day did not seem very practical. As we talked about the alternatives, it was clear that we had to either settle for a preschool we didn't feel comfortable with or move down the mountain.

Over the next few days, we prayed that God would show us His will and open the right door. As we thought about the possibility of moving, we talked about specific things that we wanted in a house and asked God to provide them. *"God if it's your will for us to move, we ask that you provide each of these things, in Jesus's name."*

During the week, Brian and I would comb the internet for homes that might fit our needs, and on Saturdays we had a realtor take us to look at them. Everything that fit our needs was either sold before we could make an offer or priced out of our range. The few homes that were available were not exactly what we wanted, and we didn't feel the peace of God over them. So, we decided to stay right where we were.

We enrolled Devin in the preschool down the mountain anyway, and hoped the Lord would make a way for us to move before the fog and snow set in.

Each day I would drop Devin off at school, and Ethan and I would drive through the neighborhood looking for any new homes that may have come on the market. I found two streets that I specifically wanted to live on, and as I drove down them I would stop my car, and pray. "God, if it's your will, open the door for us to move into this area, and we will give you all the glory."

To our surprise, in November of that year, we received a call from a couple at church who knew we were looking to move. They said that they had outgrown their home and wondered if it might fit our needs. When we went to look at it, we were blown away. It had every specific thing that we wanted, and it was in the very neighborhood, on the very street, that I had prayed for. Outside was a huge backyard with a built-in play center, a large cement pad for a basketball hoop, and a built-in barbeque. Inside was a beautiful maple wood kitchen with pull-out drawers. The master bath was a dream with a two-person shower and a separate whirlpool tub. And the best thing was, it fit our budget exactly.

We were very excited but also nervous. We knew that it was time to move, but how was I going to break the news to my parents? They loved having us near them. I knew my dad would be ok with it, but what about my mom? Would it hurt my mom if we moved away and took her only grandchildren down the mountain? Would she become depressed, and would that depression make her illness worse? My fear was that she would not handle our moving very well at all. Lying in bed that night, I asked God what I should do. "God, this looks like the right house, but is this the right time?" As I pondered, I heard a shout in my spirit that said, "Go!"

We knew that God had opened the door and that we needed to go. What we did not know was how important a step it was going to be.

The new house was a little less than a mile from the school where Devin was enrolled. Although I missed seeing my mom every morning, I knew that this was definitely the right place for us to be at that time in our life.

As time went on, my mom's health continued to deteriorate. My dad, sister, and the rest of our family were stressed and worried about her, because nothing anyone did made her feel any better.

My dad had taken her to numerous doctors, but we still had no answers about her condition. She told everyone that she just needed to rest and gain her strength back, but all she did was get weaker. What was wrong with my beautiful mother? We didn't know. Every specialist we went to threw out different opinions, and prescribed her new medication, but nothing worked. The only thing that seemed to help soothe my mother's spirit was to be close to her family.

Devin was now established in preschool, so my house was becoming easier to manage. I'm glad it was, because I really wanted to help my mom. I asked her if she would like to rest at my house while Dad was at work. I didn't like the fact that she was on the mountain all by herself, and I thought she would enjoy my company. It had been a couple months since I had seen her so I was excited to have her come over.

The next morning Dad pulled up to the house and walked my mom to the front door. I was shocked to see how much she had declined physically. She had lost an enormous amount of weight and she was already a small framed woman. Even though she had beautiful makeup on, I could see her sickness behind the mask.

She agreed that being with me would be good for her. She knew that I would pray for her and believe for her healing. I was hoping that being around her grandson everyday would give her some joy. Unfortunately, his tantrums and severe behavior continued to get worse and made it difficult for her to relax.

She would try to lie on my couch, but Ethan wouldn't leave her alone. He would stack toys on her, bounce on her, and pull her long brown hair. She remained so calm and sweet saying, "Please let Mimi rest, Ethan."

I would tell my Mom to go and lay in my bedroom, but she refused; she wanted to be with me and Ethan. Most of the day, she would just follow me around the house as if she wanted to tell me something.

After days of asking her to talk to me, she finally said, "Gina something is terribly wrong. I feel like I'm going to die." These words were like a blade to my heart.

I raised my voice and said, "No Mom, don't talk like that! You're going to live!"

Like she didn't hear me at all, she continued, "I think there is something wrong with Ethan too. I don't know what it is, but something's just not right."

"Mom, you need to lie down. You're the sick one. You need to think about your health right now. Ethan is absolutely fine. There is nothing wrong with my son."

She spent the rest of the day pacing around my house praying for Ethan. I could tell that she was overwhelmed with worry. In my heart I knew her fears about Ethan were right, but I wasn't ready to admit them.

As the weeks went by, Ethan's temper continued to worsen. When he became frustrated he would throw himself back and bang his head on the ground. This was one of the things I saw that told me maybe something really was wrong with my child. I thought after a couple bumps on his head he would stop hurting himself, but the head banging continued. Now I had to keep an even closer eye on him so he did not seriously hurt himself.

As Ethan got closer to his second birthday, we noticed even more problems. The other children at church were starting to speak and communicate with words and gestures, but he seemed to not have any interest in talking. As his behaviors worsened, he went from just hitting his head on the ground to running into and knocking over anything in his vicinity.

At church, he would purposefully run into the other kids and knock down their toys. He would climb on top of the counters, stand on the chairs and try to throw all the toys in the trash can. The teachers were concerned about his behavior and talked to us about his problems but to accommodate us they said they would assign him a personal assistant to keep him out of trouble.

One evening, we were at our music pastor's house socializing and having dinner with a few friends. The children were all together in the living room playing quietly when Ethan suddenly took off all his clothes. His clothes were thrown in every direction, and his dirty diaper went flying across the kitchen as Ethan ran through the house naked. It was things like this that always kept us on our toes.

No matter where we were, Ethan would always end up in a corner somewhere by himself. He liked to be isolated and left to play on his own. We found ourselves making excuses for the way he acted, so others would not see a problem with him. We would tell them how he talks to us at home but was very shy around others. When he acted out in anger, we would go pick him up and say, "Oh, poor Ethan must be tired, we should probably be going now."

I think I refused to accept Ethan's problems because I had always dreamed of having a perfect, healthy family, and I couldn't bring myself to admit that he might have some kind of problem. Secondly, I did not want to deal with more than one problem at a time. We were going through enough as we watched my mother's health continue to worsen.

As time went on, my mom's strength never returned. Soon, I saw my worst fears realized. My mom, my best friend, the one I had lived next to, the one I spent time with every day, the one who helped me through life, supported me in my music, and came to every one of my concerts, was gone. It was as if a part of me had died with her. While the rest of the world kept moving, my world came to a crashing halt.

I had fought hard for her during her long illness and encouraged her to do everything the doctors told her. I spent many months praying, interceding, and begging God to heal my mom, but He never did. I felt like God had let me down. I had never lost someone so close to me, and I had never fought for someone like I fought for her. Why would God take her from me? Why did she have to die so early? Why couldn't she have been here to see my kids grow up, graduate school, and get married?

After mom's funeral, I would lie in bed and ask God why she had to die. Although He never gave me an explanation, what He did tell me helped soothe my broken heart.

One night in a dream, I heard God speaking to me. I could feel the peace of God all around me. Early in the morning I woke up and wrote down what I heard. The words He spoke turned into a song that God deposited in my spirit. It's called "My Daughter."

MY DAUGHTER

I knit you together in your mother's womb
A life made so special there
    is no one like you
I have known your heart I
    have heard your cry
I have seen the dreams you have inside

My daughter, my daughter how I love you
My daughter, my daughter I will
    always be here for you
I am your father won't you
    put your trust in me
My daughter, my daughter, come to me

From the very start I've had a plan for you
Just take my hand and
    now I will walk with you
Now it is the time set your cares aside
Come to me my child I am waiting

The grains of sand on the earth
Can't compare to my many thoughts of you
Daughter know how much you are worth
You are mine

My daughter, my daughter how I love you
My daughter, my daughter
    I will always be here for you
I am your father won't you
    put your trust in me
My daughter, my daughter, come to me

Season Seven

"MRS. WALDEN, YOUR SON HAS AUTISM"

The pain of my mother's death was something I dealt with on a daily basis. I wanted to shut down and stay in bed all day long, but I forced myself to get up and keep going. Even though my world had fallen apart, life kept moving around me. So I pushed my way through each day trying to keep on being a wife to my husband and a mother to my children.

During this time, I was at church as often as possible. It was at church that my heart was most comfortable, and all my problems seemed to fade away. I found myself attending just about every service, singing and worshiping, because it was there that I found the peace that I was looking for. It was in worship that all of the stress was washed away, and I received the strength to keep moving forward.

We were at church one late September morning about a month after my mother had passed away. The previous week had been especially hard, and that day's message was just what I needed.

Pastor Jim taught on faith and believing for that which you cannot see. He asked us who we really believed in. Do we live according to the world—do we act, think, and speak according to the latest fad? Or do we believe and live according to the Word of God that never changes. I knew that I had to stop worrying and questioning God. Instead I had to look forward to His plan. I knew that although I was going through a storm, God had a plan to bring me out and use it for His glory.

Walking out of the service we felt refreshed and motivated for the week ahead. We walked over to get our kids from children's church and take them to Sunday brunch before heading home. As we arrived, two of the children's directors were waiting for us. They kindly asked to speak to us in private. I thought, *Oh no, what did Ethan do now?*

"Ethan is having difficulty paying attention and following classroom rules. He is also becoming aggressive toward the other children and we notice that his social development is far behind everyone else his age." She continued, saying, "We are not doctors or psychologists, so we can't tell you that Ethan has a special need, but we want you to be aware of his delays, so you can get him the help that he needs."

Brian did not seem to be overly worried about it, but that's him. He always takes good and bad news with a grain of salt. Nothing seems to worry him. Brian sat there holding Ethan in his lap as they told us all the things we had suspected about our son. As we sat there listening Ethan helped prove their point as he climbed all over Brian like he was a jungle gym.

Deep within, we knew that something was wrong, but this was the first time we had been confronted with it openly. I was offended and upset. I had just lost my mom and wasn't ready to deal with this yet.

As we drove home, questions flooded my mind. I knew about his problems, so why didn't I listen to my suspicions? Could I have fixed this by giving him more attention or getting him help earlier? I had to get to work and figure out how to help our son, so the very next day, I took him in to see his pediatrician.

The doctor looked him over and asked me about my concerns. Then he said, "Mrs. Walden, there are many things I see that concern me. First, Ethan seems to have a delay in language. Second, he is not responding to my voice, and third, he is not following me with his eyes.

These are all signs of autism. Unfortunately, there is really nothing that we can do about it because autism is a non-curable brain disorder."

In shock I said, "There's really nothing you can do about it? Can't you tell me how to help my son?"

He continued to say, "Mrs. Walden, I know that you're upset, but there is nothing that we can do about this. It looks like he does have autism, so you are going to have to learn to live with it. I am sorry to say, but you need to come to the realization that he most likely will never speak or communicate normally. I know this is hard, so I suggest that you and your husband seek counseling and learn how to deal with this disorder."

I felt as if someone had just punched me in the gut. I couldn't breathe, and I didn't know what to say. Then I told myself, "This doctor doesn't know my son, he has only seen him a handful of times, and he has only been in the room with us for a few minutes." My next feeling was anger; I still did not know what to do, but I was ready to kick down doors to help my son. I stood up without saying a word, picked up my child, and walked out of his office. On the way to the car, I told myself, "No doctor is going to dictate my son's future, only God will do that."

Once in the car I thought I would break down and cry, but I was too mad to cry. As I drove, I felt a strength rise up in me. I told myself that I was not going to accept this and just learn to live with it. Although I didn't know what I was going to do, I wasn't going to settle for his grim diagnosis. As I drove home I called my husband and told him what the doctor said. He agreed that the doctor did not know Ethan well enough to make that diagnosis and suggested that we should get another doctor.

As I hung up the phone, I heard a voice inside me say, *It's time to put to work that which you have sung about for so many years.* God was reminding me that the songs I had written were about faith, hope and a future; they were about believing and trusting in Him. If I wanted Ethan to be healed, then I was going to have to believe for it, speak about it, and put my faith to work to get it.

I went to bed that night with a hundred questions in my mind. The next morning, I woke up with determination to find some answers. I got on the Internet, and I looked up autism. I learned about the Inland Regional Center who was the state funded provider for children and adults with developmental disabilities. I printed out their information and was determined to call them as soon as they opened.

After getting Devin off to preschool, I started making phone calls to see who could help solve this problem. I was expecting to hear compassionate voices that were ready to help and give Ethan whatever services he needed. Instead, I was treated like another statistic.

When I called the Regional Center I was told that there was a five month waiting list to see a psychologist and get a diagnosis. I added Ethan to the list, but I had no intention of waiting five months for help.

I went back to the Internet and searched for what seemed like hours. Finally, I found an autism clinic that specialized in early childhood intervention. I was happy to see that they where in the next town not more than ten miles from my home. My frustration and anxiety turned to hope as I realized that help may be closer than I thought. I picked up the phone and called to see what they could do for my son.

"Floortime Play Center, how can I help you?"

"Hi, my name is Gina, and I think my son has autism. I'm looking for anyone that can help him get into a therapy program. I not very far away from you, so I'm hoping you can help me." My excitement quickly turned to disappointment as she said, "We don't have any openings at this time, but we will put you on our waiting list and call you as soon as a spot opens up."

This rollercoaster of emotions was tearing me up inside. All I could do was hang up the phone and cry.

I was angry and began to complain. "God, you said that all things work out for good to those that love you and are called according to your purpose. I love you, and I have followed you; I sing for you. Why my son? Why now? You know that I have been through a lot lately. Oh, Lord, I'm sorry; I should not be complaining, but I don't know how much more of this I can take.

Forgive me for complaining. I know your Word says that you will open doors that no man can open and shut doors that no man can shut, but all I'm getting is closed doors! God, I need your help! I know that you can do all things, and I need you to heal my son. I need you to show me what I need to do."

A peace came over me as I heard God say, "Keep knocking." I got up and decided that I was going to help my son beat this disorder at any cost. I was not going to give up and I would keep looking until I found someone to help us.

About an hour later, my cousin Travis and his wife Brandy showed up to check on me. I told them about all of the closed doors that I had been running into. They saw that I needed to get out of the house for a while, so I had a babysitter come over.

Travis and Brandy took me to lunch and then to a bookstore. They helped me pick out a few books on autism, so I could read up on this confusing illness. Before heading home, we decided to go and check out the Floortime Play Center that I had called earlier that day.

I was greeted at the front counter by the receptionist, "Hi, how can I help you?"

I replied, "My name is Gina, and I think my son has autism."

"Didn't I speak with you on the phone a couple hours ago?" she asked.

I burst into tears. I didn't just cry; it was like a hysterical breakdown. I did not mean to cry, but all of my emotions overcame me, and I lost it. I caused enough of a disturbance that everyone came out to see what was going on. It was embarrassing, but I couldn't help it. I was broken and did not know what to do. They tried to comfort me, but all they could do was assure me that they would call when a space became available.

When I got home, I jumped back on the computer and continued my search for more information. There were so many websites, so many therapies and so many treatments. Each one said that they would help teach my son how to live with this disorder, but I didn't want to teach him how to live with it; I wanted it to be gone completely.

In the meantime, I had a lot of choices to make. Which therapy should I choose? Which one will work best? Should I use multiple therapies? Which one had proven to help the most children? Many web pages seemed to promote one therapy over another, but I wanted to find the one that proved to work the best.

When I was at the bookstore earlier that day, I picked up a book that seemed to explain it all. It was called *The Autism Source Book*. It said,

> Intensive early-intervention maximizes a child's rate of learning and can help minimize or eliminate problem behaviors such as stimming or self-injurious behaviors. Research shows that possibly half of all children with ASDs can recover enough to develop friendships, be mainstreamed in school, have jobs and lead productive lives if they partake in early intensive intervention.

The book went on to say that "Intensive Early-Intervention" means giving a child between twenty-five and forty hours of treatment per week. This is what I was going to do. I decided that I would learn as much about autism as possible and work with my son to give him as much help as I could.

The next Sunday, on my music pastor's recommendation, I met with a mother who had two sons on the autism spectrum. Mary and I met in the foyer of the children's church and walked toward Ethan's classroom.

As we talked she asked me to tell her about Ethan. I started by saying "Ethan won't look at me, and he won't talk to me either. He becomes easily frustrated, and then he screams and throws temper tantrums. I'm also worried because he doesn't answer to his name, and he completely ignores anyone that walks into the room. I don't know if he can't hear me or if he's just ignoring me." She told me that Ethan reminded her of her own children when they were little.

"How does he act outside of the home?" she asked.

"Every time we come home, he has to touch every bush on the way into the house or he'll flip out." She told me that most children with autism have ritualistic behaviors that help them regulate their emotions. I continued to tell her that when we're out driving and I turn down a street he's not familiar with, he'll scream at the top of his lungs until I turn around. She then told me that many of these kids have trouble with changes to their routine.

"Did you ever have to pin your child down just to brush their teeth or comb their hair?" I asked.

"Every day," she answered. I continued to tell her how Ethan hated to have his hair cut so much so that I had to switch barbers every time he needed a haircut. If I went back to the same place, they'd run off and hide in the back room. She responded, "It sounds like Ethan might also have something called sensory dysfunction. You might want to look into a therapy called sensory integration."

We then walked outside to the playground so she could watch Ethan in action. As we stood there and watched the children play, she asked, "Is that your son?" She pointed right at him as I asked,

"How did you know?"

"He's the only one pacing back and forth aimlessly," she said.

We watched as the teacher called the children to line up. Everyone ran to get in line, except Ethan. He didn't even look up from what he was doing. Everyone in line looked over and watched as Ethan was dragging his body up and down the brick wall. The teacher called out for him two or three times with no response, then one of the class helpers went to get him. As she reached out to hold Ethan's hand, he pulled away from her. We watched as she tried to get Ethan to cooperate, but in response, he started yelling and bit his hand so hard it bled.

Shocked, I ran to him. I had never seen him bite himself. Mary later told me that he was probably over stimulated and didn't know how to deal with all of the noise on the playground. She was used to seeing these behaviors and told me that these were very common with autism. As church ended and we went our separate ways, she said, "With the right help and God on your side, Ethan will get better." Mary gave me some hope, and I enjoyed talking to someone who had been where I was. She made me feel like I wasn't all alone.

MORE ABOUT AUTISM

At home that week I continued to look into this disorder. I found that autism is a neurological brain disorder that affects the brain in the areas of Speech/Communication, Social Skills, Sensory Processing and Behavior.

Through all my research, I learned that no two children react to autism the same way, and it is four times more likely in boys than girls. I was shocked to also see that 1 in every 91 children are being diagnosed with this terrible disorder.

Of all the information I read that day, what stood out to me the most was this statement: *"At this time there is no cure for Autism."*

I knew that if there was no cure, then only a miracle from God could heal Ethan. As Brian and I talked that night we agreed to work together and believe for God's healing. We discussed the fact that although God can heal instantaneously, many times He chooses to work miracles through a process of obedience. Our pastor, Jim Cobrae, had taught us that if we put our faith in God and follow His direction, He would lead us down a path to our miracle. That is exactly what we were going to do. Before going to sleep that night, we prayed and asked God to lead us to the right people who would help us get our miracle.

Season Eight

THE FIGHT FOR ETHAN

One evening, not long after I had visited the Floortime Play center, I received a call from the owner. She told me that she had seen me break down in her waiting room and felt compelled to call and encourage me. She promised to make an exception and personally look into the schedule to make room for Ethan. As I hung up the phone, I felt a small amount of hope. Someone cared and was going to see if they could help. It looked like God had given me my first open door.

The next morning, I called the Inland Regional Center to see if there had been any cancellations or openings in their schedule. The answer was still, "No, but we will call you as soon as an appointment becomes available." I asked to speak to a case worker, and while holding for her one of the receptionists reminded me that, "The squeaky wheel gets the grease." She was telling me in her own way not to give up. The more I kept at them, the sooner I would get a call.

That was all that I needed to hear. Every morning, I would call them and with a friendly voice ask if there had been any openings in their schedule. I asked them to let me know whenever there was a cancellation and I would come down right away. "Until then," I told them, "I'll keep trying."

While wondering who else could help my child, I remembered hearing about a girl from church. Her name was Janelle. The church had recommended that I contact her because of she worked with young children who had developmental issues. I did not know what kind of children she worked with or what her specialty was, I just knew I had to get in contact with her.

I got her number from our church and called her right away. She was very pleasant and seemed glad to lend any assistance. Janelle wanted to know all about Ethan. She asked many questions and wanted to know about his eye contact and whether or not he responded to my voice. I would have liked to answer all of her questions, but I couldn't speak about Ethan's deficiencies. Although I had a lot to say, my emotions took over, and all I could do was cry.

Saturday morning as we agreed, Janelle came to our house to see Ethan. Brian and I watched as a tall, young lady, with long black hair and a beautiful smile walked up to our door. I was relieved and nervous at the same time. I was overjoyed that there was someone who cared enough to come and see my son, but I feared what she would say. *What will she think about him? Will she agree with the doctor, or will she see how smart he is and tell me that everything is going to be all right?*

My fears started to fade as we stood in the dining room talking about Ethan. Just by talking with Janelle for a few moments, I could see her love for children. The whole time we talked I could tell she was watching him out of the corner of her eye. "Would you like to meet him?" I asked.

"I'd love too," she responded.

We walked into the living room and watched as Ethan sat in the center of the room putting puzzles together. Before long she walked over and sat down next to him. Ethan never looked up or gave her a moment's notice; he just continued to play as if no one was near him. I saw her reach over and take one of his puzzle pieces. Initially, he did not notice, but as soon as he needed it he crawled around her and wrestled it from her hand.

After he finished, I walked over and handed him a new puzzle to work on. Janelle reached down and took another piece, but this time she held it right next to her eyes. He watched as she moved it back and forth trying to get him to look at her, but he never looked her in the eyes, he only wanted the piece of the puzzle. As she continued to interact with him, he grew frustrated, threw himself on the ground, purposefully banging his head on the tile floor. I ran over, picked him up, and helped calm him down.

I think Janelle had seen enough. I had so wanted to hear Janelle tell me that my son was going to be fine. I had hoped to show her all of his strengths but soon realized that they were that of a twelve-month-old child, not a two-year-old boy. She couldn't diagnose Ethan or tell me that he had autism, but she didn't need to; her eyes told me everything. I asked her if she could make time to help us, and to our excitement, she said she would find a couple of hours a week to work with him.

I knew that God had sent me Janelle. She was our first angel sent to help us get our miracle. Janelle showed up two times that week and started to work on engaging Ethan. Janelle's first goal was to get him to respond and acknowledge her existence.

The following week, Ethan had his first appointment at Floortime Play Center. For nearly two hours they did a full assessment on Ethan's development. The results showed that Ethan had multiple autistic behaviors as well as sensory dysfunction disorder. They showed that Ethan was also severely delayed in social and emotional growth. In fact, he was delayed in every area of development.

We were not happy to see the written proof of his results. Although we were glad that another opportunity was opening for Ethan to get the help that he needed. The Play Center recommended that we get Ethan started right away with developmental intervention, occupational therapy, and speech/language development. They told us that the earlier we got Ethan help, the better his chance for improvement.

That night, Brian and I looked over their recommendations and the cost of their program. Our health insurance would only cover twenty visits per year, so that meant after two months we would have to pay the entire cost, which was over one hundred dollars per hour. We decided that Ethan's future was worth far more than the sacrifice that it would take to pay for these services, so we decided to trust God and get him started right away.

In the meantime, I continued my daily calls to the Regional Center. A few days later, my phone rang. The lady on the other end of the phone introduced herself as Ethan's caseworker. She told me that Ethan had been assigned to her and she needed to set up an evaluation to get him enrolled in their services.

The first available appointment was three days later on a Friday morning. She told me that she would come to our house with a registered nurse and an early-intervention specialist. They would evaluate Ethan's development, give him a medical exam, and set him up as a client of the Regional Center. I was very excited to see that my daily calls had paid off. The supposed five-month wait had been cut to about three weeks.

Friday morning soon arrived, and Janelle called to tell me that she had just received her assignments for the day. I could tell that she was very excited. "What's going on?" I asked.

"I just found out that I have been assigned to be Ethan's early-intervention specialist."

"What?" I asked. "Are you kidding me?"

We were both shocked. What were the odds that Janelle would be given Ethan's case? And more so, the odds that our home would be in the exact area that she had been assigned to? Once again, I could see the hand of God working and setting up the path to Ethan's miracle. I thanked God that He led us to the exact home that we needed to be in at this time in our lives.

Since Ethan did not yet have an official autism diagnosis, the Regional Center could only give us two hours of therapy a week. But at least we were in the system, and Ethan was getting some help.

The following Monday morning, Janelle was back working with Ethan. I would make sure to sit in and learn all her techniques so I could work on engaging him throughout the day. As I had read before, I knew that an effective early-intervention program required at least twenty-five hours of engagement per week, so I made it my goal to make up the additional time myself.

As I worked with Ethan all he did was ignore me. It was then that I recognized the rejection I felt from him. I remember breaking down and crying because my own son was ignoring me. But I decided that I was not going to give up. My feelings of rejection made me want to work even harder to get through to my son.

I worked countless hours pulling him around in a wagon trying to get him to say go. I would pull him around and then stop, and I wouldn't move again until I heard him try to say something. I'd ask him, "Do you want me to go? Say go, Ethan!"

I did the same thing with the swing. I'd get him going and then stop him and make him give me a signal before I would push him again. My desire was to hear him say out loud and on purpose the word "go." One simple word, but it took a lot of work to get him to say it.

As we drove down the road, we would play the red light, green light game. At a stop light, Devin and I would try to draw it from him before we proceeded. Sometimes, I would make a safe stop in the middle of a quiet road, and wait for that word to come out of his beautiful little mouth. Again I would say, "Should we go, Ethan? Say Go!"

When I was busy with house work, or just giving Ethan a little break we kept him engaged with educational videos. Ethan loved to watch TV, so this became a useful tool in developing his language. I felt like there was no time to waste in helping him improve, so we restricted his TV time to things that were only helpful to his development.

His TV time also gave me a chance to focus on Devin. I wanted to make sure that he felt loved and needed. I never wanted him to feel left out or forgotten.

Through it all, I continued to pray. One day, I felt as if God was telling me that something in Ethan's diet needed to change. As I began to research healthy diets for autistic children, I asked God to show me what I needed to do.

I then stumbled upon a diet called *Gluten Free Casein Free* or GFCF. The information I read claimed that foods containing the proteins gluten and casein were causing multiple issues in children that had attention deficit disorder and autism. I came to find out that gluten is found in a wide variety of grains, and casein is found in dairy products. The website gave a list of common reactions that could occur; they included things like eczema, lack of attention or trouble focusing, irritability, and digestive issues. Each of these symptoms seemed to fit Ethan perfectly.

Initially, Brian thought this sounded farfetched and crazy. "How can a food that God made for our well-being cause issues in development and speech?" he asked. But as we both observed how he acted after eating, it was clear that we should look into this further.

The first thing we did was remove all dairy products including his favorite drink: cow's milk. We knew that this would be a huge challenge because Ethan loved his milk. But after he saw that there was no milk anywhere in the house, he had no choice but to drink what we gave him.

First, we tried soy milk, but Ethan's body responded to it with diarrhea. Second, we tried rice milk and then settled on almond milk. By the following week, he took to the change and an amazing thing happened: his skin started to clear up, and the dark circles around his eyes went away.

A week later, we saw an improvement in his eye contact and his language went from our favorite word "Go," to "Shake," "Choo-Choo," and "Dada." We were very excited to see some real progress in his development, and we thanked God for giving us the wisdom to make these changes.

Since we saw such an improvement by removing dairy products, we decided to go ahead and remove wheat as well. This was a lot of work; we had no idea that so many foods contain wheat as an ingredient. We could no longer feed him some of the basic foods without checking the food labels. It would be difficult, but we knew that if removing wheat was anything like removing dairy, then the rewards would far outweigh the trouble. Just as suddenly, Ethan's vocabulary started to explode with new words.

Although I was very excited at the improvements I saw in our son, I was becoming overloaded with the stresses of life. I was still trying to come to terms with the passing of my mother as well as the fact that Ethan was about to get an official diagnosis of autism.

I also worried about how all of this was affecting Devin. *Was all of the attention we were giving Ethan making Devin feel unloved and rejected?* The reality of it all this was too much for me to handle. There was not enough time or energy to give to my husband, my kids, or my own emotional health. I could feel myself fading slowly into exhaustion.

Season Nine

EXHAUSTION SETS IN

November 8th, the day after my birthday, I could barely get out of bed. As I lay there, I could hear Ethan screaming in the next room. Devin came in and said, "Mom, Ethan's screaming woke me up."

I stood up, but I couldn't move. My legs felt as if they had weights attached to them, and my arms were so heavy I couldn't lift them over my head. It was hard to breathe, and I felt as if I was going to fall over. I sat back down on the bed and thought to myself, *What is wrong with me? What time is it? I don't feel very good.* I wondered if I was having a nervous breakdown.

Once I got to Ethan's room, I could barely pick him up. I stumbled to the phone and called my sister who came right over and took me to the emergency room. After many tests, blood work, and a physical assessment, they determined that nothing was wrong with me. The doctor said, "It looks like you just need some rest." He continued to tell me that after physical or mental trauma your body needs time to recover."

I went home and got in bed, but I couldn't shut my mind off. For the next few days, I felt no different. Every morning, I woke up to the same symptoms. I so wanted to stay healthy and avoid running to the doctor, but I really felt like something was seriously wrong with me.

By the end of the week, I had been in the ER three times. By the third visit, I realized that there was nothing physically wrong with me. Deep inside, I still wanted them to admit me so I could get some sleep. Once again they sent me home, and told me to get some rest.

I got a few hours sleep that night, when suddenly, I was awakened with fear and panic. I saw an image of a man in our hallway looking into Ethan's bedroom.

Was this real or a hallucination? Were my eyes playing tricks on me, or was this sickness standing at his door?

I can't tell you for sure, but I jumped out of bed and ran full speed into Ethan's room. As I reached the room, I stumbled and tripped over the baby gate and ended up on his bedroom floor in tears. Brian came running in after hearing me crash over the gate.

"What's going on?" he said. "What's wrong? What are you doing?"

As I cried, he held me in his arms and told me everything was going to be all right. Brian prayed over me, our boys, and our home, and then led me back to bed.

Lying there, I realized this is what happens when one tries to deal with life's issues their own way. As I talked to God, I asked Him to take over and open the doors that needed to be opened and shut the doors that needed to be shut. I asked Him to give me wisdom on how to help my son. I prayed that He would show me how to rely on His strength and how to live under His amazing Grace. I told

God that I was not going to make one more move in my fight for Ethan until I heard a Word from Him.

Later that night, I woke up and heard God's voice so loud in my spirit that it almost seemed audible. I heard Him say, "He will speak. He will tell the goodness of God. It will happen."

Those words soothed my soul and brought peace to my inner being. I got up and I wrote them all over our house. I posted them on the walls, hung them on the refrigerator, and told everyone I knew what God had told me.

It was that day that Brian and I realized this fight for our son was as much a spiritual one, as it was physical. We needed to seek God for the answers to this problem, and we needed to believe the words that He spoke.

God showed me that I needed to speak life over Ethan in spite of the problems that I saw. From then on, as Ethan sat in his highchair eating, I would speak over him.

I told him, "Don't worry, Ethan, you will speak. You will tell the goodness of God; it will happen!" Throughout the day I would tell him, "You will have friends; you will go to school; you can be anything you want to be; everything's going to be okay."

Although he stared off into space and didn't seem to notice, I knew that his spirit could hear me, so I continued to tell Him that God was going to heal him.

Even though we were continually reminded of his problems, Brian and I chose to speak life and hope over him because we knew that God had a plan and a purpose for his life.

The next morning, I woke up and found that Brian had printed out scripture and posted them all over the house. One of them was Jeremiah 29:11. I remember that my grandmother had given me that same verse for Ethan.

When Ethan was still very young, she told me that God had given her that verse for him. She even wrote his name right next to it in her Bible to remind her of what God had shown her. As I thought back, I remember her telling me how important it was to speak the Word of God over your life and how powerful it was to sing it and proclaim it over your family.

Because music came easily to me, I put melody to the scripture and began singing the Word of God over my family. This is one of those songs that I wrote while reading Psalms 27.

ROCK OF
MY SALVATION

The Lord is my light and my salvation
Whom shall I fear
The Lord is my strength
the lifter of my head
I will not be afraid
The enemy may come against me
He will stumble and fall
Though my foes may come to harm me
I will not be moved at all

Jesus you're the Rock of my Salvation
There is no one like you
Jesus you're the Rock of my Salvation
There is no one like you, Jesus

Jesus how great you are
Jesus how great you are

We wanted our attitude and our focus to be on the Word of God and on what He said, not on what we saw. We would not allow ourselves to dwell on the negative or complain any longer about our predicament. We chose to worship and praise God for what we knew He was going to do. It was not always easy, and though I still had occasional breakdowns, I quickly got back up and started to thank God.

Each time I sang in church, I would praise God like He had already healed my son. I knew that the manifestation was on the way; it was in the works. It had been set forth. I soon realized that I would rather be in the storms of life with God than in the sunshine all alone.

I remember back to when Pastor Jim taught us that what we see and hear may be the reality in front of us, but it will only dictate your future if we let it. He said, "Only the Word of God is true; His Word is what we must believe in. We must look past our situations and issues and trust God to work out His promises in us."

I was reassured that God does have a plan and a purpose for our lives, and God has written a destiny for each of us. It seemed like it took me a long time to learn, but I had finally come to a place where I chose to believe God's Word more than reality itself.

It was still hard to hear the opinions of people and see the reality of life and look past it, but that is what we chose to do. We believe that God is more powerful than any diagnosis or medical professional, and we knew that He had the final word over our son. No matter what life was going to throw at us, we knew that our God is stronger, higher, and more powerful than life itself.

Even though I choose to believe God I still wondered if I was doing everything I could. When the boys were in bed and the house was quiet, I would ask myself if I was doing everything I could for my son.

One night I heard God say, "Be quiet, just be quiet, and listen to what I have to say."

After many nights crying out to Him and hearing nothing, it was in the silence that I was able to actually hear God. I realized that if I never stopped my mind from questioning that it would be impossible to hear God speak.

I quickly learned to take my cares and requests to God and then be quiet until He answered. I longed for that quiet place, just sitting at the feet of the Most High in worship. I found this to be the place where healing truly begins.

Right there in His presence, I saw many visions in my spirit. Once I saw Ethan in a kindergarten class interacting with normal-functioning children. He was talking and laughing and learning in a regular education classroom. I held onto that as a promise, and I knew in my spirit that by the age of five, Ethan would be well.

I would have liked God to reach down and touch my son and heal him instantaneously, as I know He can, but God had a different plan in mind. He wanted me to walk down the road of faith and believe for something that I could not yet see. He wanted me to put my faith into action and believe for my son. As Brian and I walked down this road, we can now say that we have both learned invaluable life lessons that have changed us forever.

OH MOST HIGH

Oh most High
I have come into your Glory
I humbly kneel at your feet
I'm healed before your throne

Oh most High,
All the angels cry you're worthy,
Wonderful, beautiful, enthroned in Majesty

Holy, Holy, the Lord God Almighty
Creator of all things
Holy, Holy, surrounded by your Glory
My eyes have seen the King.

Oh Most High,
Majesty the Lord of Glory
I fall down, I lay my crown
Before the King of Kings

Oh Most High
Lamb of God the great Almighty
Crucified, now glorified
You reign in victory

Season Ten

On November 17, 2006, Ethan had his appointment to see the psychologist at Inland Regional Center. In preparation, I gathered all of his medical records and his developmental reviews from his therapists. Even though most people do not want their child labeled with this terrible disorder, I wanted it. I know it sounds crazy, but I knew that in order to get Ethan the services that he needed, it would take me accepting the reality of his condition.

As I sat in the waiting room, I saw families with children who were blind, others who couldn't speak, a few had Down syndrome, and many were there for the same reason I was. All of the commotion and noise was deafening. It was definitely too much for Ethan; it even proved to be too much for me.

As I tried to keep him calm, he started screaming and yelling and throwing his body around. I struggled to hold him still, all the while wondering if he would break my nose or knock out my teeth with the back of his head. I tried books, crayons, and even a video game, but nothing would calm him down. At one point he got away from me and ran down the hall. I chased after him wishing we could keep running right out the front door. We were almost out of the building. I reached him; I picked him up, held him in my arms, and took him back to the waiting room.

Nearly an hour later it was our turn. We were taken into a room with one small desk and a few toys on the floor. The psychologist followed us in and handed me a four-page questionnaire about Ethan's behaviors. As I filled it out, she took a few minutes to try and interact with him. I then handed her Ethan's papers and medical records, and I told her that I knew Ethan had autism. "I need the diagnosis so I can get him the help he needs." After looking through his records and assessing him, she agreed, and Ethan received a diagnosis of Moderate to Severe Autistic Disorder.

Although I really wanted it, the reality of the diagnosis sent shockwaves of emotion through me. At home I reacted just like the first time I realized Ethan had autism.

I so wanted to talk to my mom. So I picked up the phone and began dialing her number! Just then I remembered, *I can't, she's gone.* I hung up the phone, fell to my knees, and cried. Oh how I needed to talk to her; she always had a way of making me feel better.

I thought to myself, *Maybe I can call my dad. He could always fix anything. No, I better not. I can't burden him with this pain. I don't think he could handle it right now.*

So there I was, all alone with my problems. During the day I learned how to manage them, but in the quietness of the night, my fears, worries, and thoughts would overwhelm me.

Brian would quickly fall asleep leaving me to worry all by myself. Even though he was beside me, I felt like I was all alone. I thought to myself, *Am I the only one worried about our son? Does Brian even care? I know he cares; he's just too busy with work. I know he's trying hard to cover all these costs. I know he's tired, but I wish he would take more time to talk to me.*

Over time, we learned to sit down together and talk about our day. We learned about the importance of what our church called *Safe Talk*. They encouraged us to put the kids to sleep and make time to talk about our feelings. This was hard in the beginning, but with practice it helped bring us closer in our marriage and our parenting.

Even though we were talking more, there were still nights where I was battling the reality of Ethan's diagnosis all by myself. One night Satan was throwing questions of doubt into my mind. He said, "Is God really going to heal your son? Look at all his problems, there's no way out of it. This diagnosis is going to define him for the rest of his life. He'll never be potty-trained; I bet he'll be in diapers all his life. And by the way, if God didn't heal your mom, how do you know He's going to heal your son?"

When I heard that last one, I had heard enough. I responded, "Get behind me Satan, and go back to hell where you belong. You've been defeated, and you have no right to speak into my life. You're a liar, so don't waste your time talking to me. I don't receive a word of it! And you know what? This battle is not mine, it's God's, and He's already won. As for my mom, to be absent from the body is to be present with the Lord, so in the end, she won, too."

In my mind, I saw a picture of Satan running off with his tail between his legs. From that night on, I no longer had battles in my mind or sleepless nights of fear or worry.

Brian and I reminded each other to speak the word of God over any problems and issues that came up in Ethan's life. We would say, "By His stripes Ethan is healed," (1 Peter 2:24); "My God will never leave me nor forsake me," (1 Kings 8:47); "If God is for me, who can be against me," (Romans 8:31), and "Greater is He that is in me, and in Ethan, than he that is in the world," (1 John 4:4). As we did this, it became easier to believe God for Ethan's healing.

We stood on the fact that God's Word is true, and He can not lie. His promises are yes and amen, and that was what we were going to believe and stand on.

As we sat in church one Sunday morning, I was again reminded that we overcome by faith and the word of our testimony. It was then, that I decided I was going continue to speak out in faith and tell everyone what I had seen in my spirit.

Monday morning while Ethan was in therapy, I sat down and wrote this e-mail:

> To all my friends and family,
>
> As you all know, we have been going through some very difficult times with the recent passing of my mother and now with my son's behavior and developmental issues. My worst fears were confirmed a few days ago when Ethan and I sat in front of a psychologist and received a diagnosis of moderate to severe autism.

We have been told that autism is a non-curable brain disorder, but we are choosing to stand in faith for our son and believe for his healing. God has shown me that He is going to use this trial to show us His goodness, His mercy, and His grace. We believe that Ethan will be well by the age of five. What Satan has meant for evil, God will turn around and use it for good. Not only will this child speak and prove the doctors wrong, he will one day be used to impact nations for God.

I ask you all to stand in faith with me, and pray for us as we walk through this season of life.

Ethan will speak; he will tell the goodness of God; it will happen. Just wait and see.

Gina

Season Eleven

LOTS OF WORK AHEAD

Now that Ethan had an official diagnosis of Autism, the Regional Center was able to increase his therapy from two hours, to fifteen hours a week. He also qualified for an additional hour of speech and an hour of occupational therapy per week. In addition, we were offered something called respite care. Respite care is a service that allows the family to hire a family member or friend to watch their child while they get away for a few hours each week. We were very happy to finally get the added services as well as the blessing of free babysitting.

Although Janelle had a full workload, she was able to somehow fit the extra thirteen hours we were given into her schedule. Soon she realized that she could not keep up with this schedule and put in a request to find an additional therapist.

About two weeks later we found Amy. We soon realized God had sent us another angel. Janelle and Amy were not just great with Ethan, they were also a great help and support to me. They taught me how to look past Ethan's disability and see his abilities. They taught me how to engage my son and love him for who he was. Not only were they great teachers, they also shared my belief in God. Brian and I knew that God had sent these two girls. Both strongly believed that with God, indeed all things are possible; even the healing of a non-curable brain disorder!

Once we had confirmation of full time in-home therapy, Brian took out a second mortgage on our house and used the money to turn our two-car garage into a therapy center. He bought a shed and moved all of our stuff outside. He put drywall up, painted the entire room, and had wardrobe-like closets put across both walls. We filled them with all sorts of toys, puzzles, books and balls. Then we bought floor mats and covered the floor with a soft play surface, and we put up four swing brackets so the boys could swing together no matter what the weather was like outside. One of the swings we put up was a special spandex swing that Ethan could get inside of, so we could swing, bounce, and spin him in circles. This became Ethan's private therapy room that was used every day of the week.

Each morning Ethan would wake up, eat breakfast, and then join one of his therapists in the garage for his morning session. Ethan and I would go to one of the many fast food restaurants for lunch on the way to Floortime Play Center. Then we would return home for our afternoon session.

Each day I was happy to see Janelle's blue min-van drive up to the house. It meant help was here, and I could learn how to continue reaching my son. Janelle always came with a beautiful smile on her face. She brought joy into the house the moment she walked in.

I would open up the garage, and there she was holding bags of toys for Ethan to play with. She brought many different things to his therapy hoping to catch his interest.

One day, she brought a play barn with many farm animals. Ethan had been showing an interest in animals so she thought she might give this a try. She spread out the play set and took out the farm animals one by one to show Ethan. She would make animal sounds as each animal peaked out of the bag. She was very animated with her voice and facial expressions as she tried to catch Ethan's attention. He stared at the bag intently, and you could see he was wondering what was going to happen next. Once all of the animals were out, Janelle began to place them into the barn for some pretend play. As she set them down, Ethan would snatch them away and put them in his own pile.

I knew exactly what he was going to do. He was going to line them up in perfect order, just as he does his food, his books, and all of his toys. I think lining things up made him feel in control and organized. He did just as I assumed, placing each animal next to the other by height.

Janelle sat back and let him do his organizing. As soon as he was done, she was back trying to engage him. She was getting to know Ethan, so she knew she had to let him have his ideas too. She crawled over to him and said, "Look at all of your animals standing so nicely in that line!"

At that point, he became very frustrated because she was invading his space. He then began knocking them over. She stayed very calm and said, "Oh, look the animals are laying down. Are they sleeping? Night, night, little farm animals." I was so impressed with how she handled him, and her sweet soothing voice helped Ethan calm down.

The next thing we heard was a knock on the garage door. Amy was here to team teach with Janelle. Amy and Janelle work well together, and I knew she would have some ideas to help engage him in play.

Amy came in, said hello and jumped right into the session. "Hey Ethan, I love animals, can I play?" She sat on the carpet right next to Janelle and gently pulled a mama horse from the pile. She then galloped the horse around the farm saying, "Neigh! Neigh!"

Janelle took the cue and joined in with the daddy horse. They were running around the garage, stopping every few minutes to eat a pretend apple. Amy and Janelle were modeling what play looks like, because kids with autism usually don't understand the concept.

Ethan had gone back to lining his animals, but I could see by the look on his face that he was listening and observing their actions. Amy then walked the mama horse over to Ethan's line up of animals and said "Hey, have any of you farm animals seen my baby? I can't find my baby!" She galloped the mama horse through the farm and around the stable looking for the baby.

Ethan watched her as she galloped off. Then I saw him scan his line of animals. *Is he going to respond to her request?* I thought. *Is he looking for the baby horse?*

Ethan reached down, picked up the baby horse, and without a sound galloped the little horse over to his mama. I froze in shock, Ethan had just responded! I watched him as he took the baby and fed it some pretend apples, and then followed the momma horse around the garage. I couldn't wipe the smile off my face; Ethan was pretend playing!

We were all ecstatic with his progress. He was listening and he was learning. We knew there was a little boy locked inside of autism. He wanted out and he wanted to play. With God's help, we knew there would be more great progress to come.

Over the next few weeks, Ethan's language started to develop. One morning just after breakfast, I sat down with him to look through a picture book. As I pulled him into my lap, he looked at the book and touched each picture. As he put his finger on each of the twelve animals he spoke out their names.

My mouth fell open in shock; he had never before identified the names of these animals, or spoke that many words at one time. It was as if God had touched his tongue and opened his mouth to speak. Tears formed in my eyes as I listened to Ethan speak these brand new words.

Ethan, you did it! You knew every animal! I was so proud of his new accomplishment.

Although the improvements we saw since getting Ethan help, and changing his diet, were amazing, there were still many problem areas we needed to work on. I remember one day I left Ethan to watch one of his DVDs, while I went to put away a load of clean clothes. When I came in to check on him, he was not where I had left him. I found him in the kitchen with the refrigerator doors wide open and all of the items lined up across the kitchen floor. Each item was lined up by height and color. Although his work was very creative and I didn't mind someone cleaning out my refrigerator, this was not what I had in mind.

I put everything back into the refrigerator and returned him to the TV. A little later, I came back to check on him and again found him on the kitchen floor, sitting next to nicely lined items of refrigerated foods. After many days of the same behavior, we added a safety lock so he could no longer get in the refrigerator by himself.

Ethan was also a runner. We had to hold his hand or carry him anytime we went outside. If he saw something that interested him, he would take off and run toward it. He gave no thought to oncoming traffic or any other dangers in the area. He just wanted to get to whatever he was looking at. Although he was still limited in his vocabulary, we could tell that his mind was always busy looking for something that might catch his interest.

One morning after I dropped Devin off at school, I returned home to meet my sister. We sat at the table drinking our coffee, while Ethan was in his room playing with toys. Just then, my neighbor came over to tell me that their car had been broken into and to keep an eye out for anyone suspicious. Somehow during that conversation, Ethan walked right by me and wandered out the front door. It must have been four or five minutes before we noticed that he was gone. My sister and I frantically looked all over the house, checked the backyard and his therapy room, but all to no avail. We went out front, running from door to door, asking if anyone saw him. We were going crazy. Where did Ethan go? How could this have happened? Just as we were about to call the police, my sister saw a small child about a block away. He was standing in the middle of our busy street with nothing but a diaper on. In panic, we ran as fast as we could, yelling for him. It was not until I grabbed him and held him tight that he noticed me and said, "Momma."

Situations like this one, taught us how to think creatively. We had to always stay one step ahead of him to keep him safe. We also learned to look ahead and see what might set him off and cause a meltdown. Regardless of where we were, we learned to look for anything that might be dangerous. He was always putting things in his mouth, climbing on top of, and jumping off anything in his reach.

Even though things were getting better, with each new morning there was a different challenge to deal with. One morning after getting the boys dressed and ready to walk out the door, Ethan walked out of the hallway completely naked. "Ethan, what are you doing?" I asked. "I just got you dressed, and we need to get Devin to school." He didn't answer or say a word. Instead he took off running through the house. This continued every day that week until we figured out that certain clothes irritated him. Things like tags scratched against his skin and drove him crazy, so we had to find clothing that didn't bother him. Through it all, Ethan taught us to never take a moment of silence for granted.

The next Sunday, after a long, hard week we went to both the morning and the evening services at church. That night, the pastor talked to the men about being the priest of their homes and learning to cover their wives and children in prayer. He challenged men to rise up and be the leaders of the home and to teach their families about God by their example.

God was using this message to speak to Brian. He knew that he needed to go home, and as the priest of the home, anoint Ethan with oil and dedicate him to the Lord. It would be different from when we stood in front of the church to officially dedicate him to the Lord. This needed to be done with a heart of faith and a sincere cry for mercy by the man of the house.

On the way home, the children fell asleep. We carried them in the house, and tucked them into their beds, praying over them like we did every night.

Just before we turned in for the night, Brian said he wanted us to go pray for Ethan again. He went and found a bottle of olive oil, and then we knelt next to Ethan's bed.

Brian touched his head with oil and prayed, "Lord, I pray that Ethan would grow up to know you personally and that out of these lips he would speak about your goodness and proclaim your healing to the nations." He touched his feet and said, "That his feet would walk in your ways." Then he took Ethan in his hands and lifted him up over his head, "And Lord we ask for Ethan's healing, from the top of his head to the bottom of his feet; we ask that you would show your power in him and use him for your glory. We thank you for what you are going to do, for what only you can do. Amen."

As Brian and I got back into bed, we reminded each other of the importance of believing for God's promises and not allowing the circumstances in front of us to get into our spirit. Even though we saw the issues and problems of autism, we had to continue to choose to believe for healing and hold on to what God had shown us. As we talked, we encouraged each other to believe that God's Word is more powerful than the situations and reality in front of us.

The truth is, the reality of daily life did affect us both. It made us feel weak in faith. Even though Ethan was making great progress, I seemed to focus more on the problems that he still had and less on the improvements that he was making. When I allowed myself to focus on those problems and relive them in my mind, worry, stress, and fear would overtake me. But as I changed my focus from my problems to God's promises, I could hear God remind me to be still, to trust Him, and to know that He is God.

It is God's word that brought peace to my soul and clarity to my mind, and it is God's word that helped me establish my faith in the promises that he gave to me. During these times of mental and physical battle, God showed me how to use His Word to still the worry of my mind and trust him.

I wrote a lot of songs during these times. This next song, not only became a prayer to God, but also a declaration of my trust in Him.

I WILL BE STILL

Where am I going
My vision is blurring
Which way was I supposed to go
My plans they are failing
My direction is changing
For the first time I don't know
I feel like just running away
        from all this pain
But I lift my eyes to the hills

I will be still and know you're God
I will be still and know you're God
Seasons of my life may change
But Lord your promise stays the same
I will be still and know you're God
I will be still and know you're God

My head raised to heaven
I look for the Son
I can see your light through my tears
You said you wouldn't give me
        more than I can bear
I know that you won't leave me here
I feel like just running away
        from all this pain
But I lift my eyes to the hills

You promised me Lord
You'd never leave me
I'm not alone, So I'll keep believing
With all of my heart, I put
    my life in your hands

I will be still and know you're God
I will be still and know you're God
Seasons of my life may change
But Lord your promise stays the same
I will be still and know you're God
I will be still and know you're God

Season Twelve

Although finances were very tight, every Saturday after-noon when Brian got home from work, we would use our respite care for date nights. I would put on makeup, do my hair, and put on a nice outfit just like I would do before we got married. When we didn't have the money for a nice restaurant or even a movie, we would go to the park and have a picnic or just go for a walk around a golf course. It didn't matter what we did; we just needed to get away from the children and from the trials of autism for a few hours. Over the last few years I had forgotten how much fun being with my husband really was.

This time together probably saved our marriage. It is well documented that over eighty-five percent of couples end up divorced when their child is diagnosed with a mental or developmental problem. Brian and I were determined that this was not going to happen to us. We used these date nights to stay connected and keep a healthy marriage.

In addition to our own time away, we also took time to make Devin feel special. One Saturday a month we made sure to take him on a special date to give him the attention he deserved.

My other avenue of escape was church. Brian and I were at church as much as we could be. Church was the place we went to get refreshed and refocused for the days ahead. On Tuesday evenings, Brian taught a men's group and we made sure to never miss a Wednesday night service. Then, on Thursday evenings I had choir practice, and every other weekend I would help lead worship at all four services. I always looked forward to getting to church and into the presence of God. It was during praise and worship that I could truly rest in the arms of God.

In worship is where I would find peace and grace for whatever might lay ahead. It was also comforting to know that the boys were well-looked after. I knew that the teachers in children's church had cared for Ethan since birth, and they would protect him and take care of him like their own.

As we sat in church, we heard our pastor teach us that grace is God's sovereign divine ability to get the job done on our behalf when we can't do it. That really spoke to me, because I knew that I could not do this on my own. I could not heal Ethan, and I didn't know what steps to take to make him better.

I use to run to my dad to fix everything, and then Brian loved to solve whatever problems arose, but neither of them could fix Ethan.

The only thing we could do was trust and rely on God. He is the only one that we knew could perform miracles. Not only had I read about the healing power of God in the Bible; Brian and I had seen it with our own eyes.

I've always wondered why God heals some people instantly, but others He takes on a path that lead them to their healing. Then with some, like my mom, he chooses not to heal at all.

Frankly, I don't know; I doubt any of us really do. But one thing the Word of God has taught us is if you and I walk with God and trust Him with all of our hearts, He will never leave us nor forsake us, and He will always do what is best for us.

> But blessed is the one who trusts in the lord,
> whose confidence is in him. They will be like
> a tree planted by the water that sends out its
> roots by the stream.
>
> Jeremiah 17:7-8a

Season Thirteen

THE FIRST IEP

Just before Ethan turned three, we received a letter in the mail asking us to call and make an appointment to see the school psychologist, speech pathologist, and the school nurse. The letter stated that at three years of age the school district takes over as the provider of services, and they needed these reports to prepare him for the upcoming IEP. The letter defined an IEP as an individual education plan, which is a legally binding agreement between the parents and the school district that lays out his education plan for the following year.

Out of frustration I thought, *We just got Ethan's home program set up, and I just got my foot in the door with the Regional Center, and now the school district is going to take over?* I wondered what the school district was going to offer us, and if they would take away our home program and put him in a special education classroom.

I didn't know what to do, but fortunately I had met some parents that had already been through this process. My friend Mary, for instance, not only had two boys on the autism spectrum, she was also a special education teacher. She was able to help familiarize us with the special education laws and showed us how every special education child has a right to be educated in the least restrictive environment. I came to find out that this meant Ethan could even be enrolled in a non-disabled class, next to non-disabled peers.

Prior to Ethan's IEP, we scheduled and completed the required evaluations. At each one, I asked what options and placements were available. In addition I asked what recommendations they were going to make for him. They told me that the school district had developed a special education preschool program, and they thought Ethan would be a perfect fit for the class.

Something about a special education class did not settle right with my spirit. I thought, *How can a child learn, grow, and graduate out of special education when all he or she sees and knows is special education?* I did not want this for my son. I wanted to keep what we had at home because I could tell that it was working.

All we could do was prepare, pray, and hope that the school district would agree with our request and keep Ethan in his home program. In preparation for the IEP, we put together all the goals that we had made and the improvements that he had shown in the last five months. We placed them all neatly in a folder for each person who was scheduled to be at the meeting.

On the front, we printed a full-page picture of our son. We wanted to put a face in front of everyone at the meeting and show them that this was more than another IEP about a child with autism. We were showing them, that as his parents, we were going to be involved in every area of his education.

On the second page, we typed out a quote that I had seen. It said, "Most parents are told to prepare their child for an institution; we're planning for Harvard." That quote spoke to my heart and reminded me that there are no limits to what you can be or who you can become. We wanted to show everyone at the meeting that we had a plan, and we needed their help and their resources to give Ethan the best chance at success. The rest of the folder was made up with Ethan's test scores and the current recommendations from his therapists.

The morning of the IEP, we dressed in our best business attire. We were serious about this meeting and knew that the outcome would determine Ethan's academic direction for years to come. I was nervous to go in and sit down with this group of seasoned professionals, as I really didn't know much about this diagnosis. It almost felt like I had to go from being a mom who had never heard about autism, to a knowledgeable autism specialist overnight.

Before walking in, we stopped and prayed. We asked God to be our advocate and asked Him to help us say the right things that would lead us to the right outcome. I felt a peace come upon me as I heard God tell me, "Gina, just handle this just like you do your singing. Go in there, push your shoulders back, and when you open your mouth, I will give you the right words to say."

As we walked in, we were greeted by eight professionals sitting around a large table, ready to give us their opinions about our son. Only a few of those at the table had even met Ethan; the rest where school officials and department heads that were there to introduce us to the school district and make sure we were well informed of their role in Ethan's education.

Once we had all introduced ourselves, Brian and I proceeded to hand each of them an Ethan folder. As they opened them, we witnessed various emotions on there faces.

One smile seemed to say, *Wow, it's nice to see parents who care about their child;* another had a look of *What is going on here? These people are taking over our meeting.* Across the table was a look of *Oh no, we're going to be here a while.*

Brian then turned everyone's attention to page three of our folder which was entitled *Parent Concerns.* The page stated that although Ethan had a diagnosis of moderate to severe autism, our goal for him was by the age of five to be educated in a regular kindergarten classroom next to non-disabled peers. It must have been hard for them to grasp our goals for Ethan's future, because they did not line up with the reality of his diagnosis. It was obvious that some of them thought we didn't understand the seriousness of Ethan's condition. But we did. They just didn't realize that we had a word from God and a plan and hope for his future. We just needed the school district to get on board and help us achieve it.

Brian and I took turns going over every assessment with the team, showing them the test results when he enrolled in each program, and the progress that he had made so far. We made sure they knew that even though he was far behind, he was making amazing improvement. After going through the folder with them, I closed by asking them to provide the funding for us so we could continue our intensive, early-intervention home program.

The room was silent. They looked at us like we were the craziest parents they had ever met with. I expected this reaction and knew coming in that talking them into keeping our home program would not be easy.

The psychologist then ruffled through his papers and read us Ethan's diagnosis, as if we had never heard it before. He continued to say, "Mr. and Mrs. Walden, I'm not sure you realize the severity of this disorder. These types of cases do not get better. Autism is a non-curable brain disorder, although Ethan may improve in some areas, this is not something your child is going to outgrow completely. According to these test results, Ethan is nowhere close to being ready for a mainstream classroom."

We listened politely but remained confident in what God had showed us. We knew where they were coming from, but we were not going to accept anything other than God's promises. None of them were aware of the immovable promise we had received from the Great Physician.

In response I said, "My husband and I are positive that if we continue the home program Ethan will continue to improve. And when he is developmentally and academically ready we will slowly integrate him into a classroom setting."

The principal of the school kindly handed us some literature on his program. He said that a lot of parents are in denial when they're faced with a diagnosis of this kind. He assured me that he had worked with these kids for years, and he would make sure Ethan would be cared for and continue to learn. I could tell that he had a great heart and that he took good care of his students—but this student was not going to be one of them.

We truly did appreciate all of their input; however, we were Ethan's true professionals, and we knew what he needed. I told them there was no way anyone could spend

BRIAN & GINA WALDEN

fifteen minutes with our son and claim to know what's best for him.

Again we asked the school district to keep and fund the program that Ethan had at home. Finally, one of them stated that they did not have a contract with the agencies that Ethan was enrolled with so keeping the home program would be impossible.

Brian then asked to talk to the person who had the authority to set this up, and the response was "There is no such person."

They again made us aware of what they could provide by saying, "The district has developed a special preschool class for children like Ethan. The class is held from 8:30 a.m. to12:30 p.m. every day of the week, and we can arrange to pick up your son and transport him to and from school. Each class is trained and equipped to teach your son and deal with any issues that may arise."

We were at a roadblock; it looked like there was no way that we were going to come to a agreement that day.

After nearly three hours of discussion, we ended our meeting and parted ways. Before we left, they principle asked us to come by the school and sit in on the class. I think they hoped we would change our minds once we saw their class in action.

Three days later, my sister and I showed up to sit in on one of the classes. My heart broke for all of the children. Some of them wore helmets on their heads, others were rolling around on the floor, and some were chewing on their clothing instead of paying attention to the teachers. There was one teacher and one assistant doing their best to teach all of the children, but there was not a lot they could do. I am sure they were capable teachers doing the best that they could, but I asked myself, *How can two individuals teach all of these children who have so many different problems?* I could not see how anyone could learn in this type of environment.

Brian and I were convinced that a one-on-one home program would be the only way to help Ethan prepare for general education classes. We feared that if Ethan was in a class with other disabled students, he would mimic them and pick up more severe behaviors.

We felt that it was important for Ethan to have non-disabled peers to learn from, so we decided that our son would not be included in any disabled program. It is not that we looked down on any of these children or thought the program was not helpful; it's just that our son did not belong there. If he was going to grow out of special education, he needed to be around kids that he could learn normal behavior from.

A few days after we visited the class, I spoke to the director of special education. I could tell that I was not going to get her to agree with me and allow us to keep our home program, so we had to look at other options.

Brian went to the Internet and looked into the laws as they pertained to special education. He found that every child with special needs has certain rights under the Individuals with Disabilities Education Act of 2004 (IDEA 2004). The California Department of Education website said that during an IEP, if the school district and the parents or guardians cannot reach an agreement as to a Free and Appropriate Public Education under Section 504 for Students with Disabilities, then we were to send a letter describing the problem and the disagreement to the California Special Education Department.

That letter would then be read and reviewed by a judge, and if the complaint was determined as credible, a due process case would be started. So that is what we did.

At the time we had no idea what a due process case was. We soon found out when we received a package in the mail that read across the top "Ethan Walden versus the School District."

To our shock, we had unintentionally started a lawsuit with the school district for not providing a "Free and Appropriate Education environment."

We were pleased to see that the Due Process lawsuit put a freeze in Ethan's current program. This meant that until we reached an agreement, we could keep all current services in place.

Brian read through the paper work and realized that we were in over our heads. He suggested that we call and get some legal help.

I called Ethan's caseworker at the Regional Center to ask for their recommendation and to see if they had any legal assistance that they could offer us. I was told that they did have a special education advocacy department to assist in these matters, and I should contact them.

Unfortunately, we learned that there was only one advocate and she had a four month backlog, so they would not be available to give us immediate assistance.

In frustration, I said to myself, "What do I do now? Who else can I call?"

A friend then told me if I could find an attorney that had a contract with the Regional Center then we could apply for a grant to cover the costs. That was great news; *we might be able to get an attorney that we don't have to pay for.* Brian and I looked through a list of special education attorney's in our area and I called each one to see if any had a contract with the Regional Center.

The following week, we agreed to meet with the only one that called us back. After filling out our paperwork, a tall, well-dressed man in his early forties greeted us and asked us to follow him to his office. I noticed that his left arm was in a sling. Brian and I looked at each other, wondering what happened. We sat down in two comfortable chairs and looked at his large bookcase full of law books lined up in alphabetical order. As he reviewed our case, compassion came over me. I realized that his arm wasn't hurt, it was a prosthetic. Maybe this man became a special education attorney because he knew from experience the issues that our children have to deal with.

"Tell me about your disagreement with the school district and how I can help you." We showed him all of the test results that we presented to the IEP team, and shared with him our goals for Ethan's future, and our hope for his complete recovery.

He was impressed by all of the work that we had done and how hard we were fighting for our son. He stated that most parents are happy to take anything they can get just so they can to get some help. It took about a half an hour for him to review all the information. He then looked up at us and said, "I agree that a special education class would not be the best placement for Ethan's development and may even cause regression."

He informed us that he would take the case and write a letter of representation to the school district and the State Board of Education. We left his office overjoyed. We now had professional representation to help get Ethan what he needed.

A few days later, we received a letter informing us of the dates for a resolution meeting, and if needed, a due process hearing. The following week, we were surprised to receive a certified letter from the school district informing us that the director of special education would like to meet with us and work on a compromise.

We were able to schedule a meeting the very next week. On one side of the table sat my husband, my sister, me, and our attorney. Across from us sat a well-dressed professional lady who introduced herself as the director of special education.

Our attorney explained that because of Ethan's sensory overload issues, a classroom environment would prove to be an obstacle and not a benefit to his learning. He continued to show her the progress that Ethan had made at home and then explained our plan to get him preschool ready. After hearing our concerns and seeing our goals the Director agreed with us and called in her receptionist to write up an agreement for continuation of in-home services.

We had won. We knew that we needed to keep our home program, but we could have never kept it without the help of a qualified attorney on our side. God knew the desires of our heart and as His Word says, He made it all work together for good.

The disagreement was behind us; God had again made a way. Everything worked out and even through the change of service providers; we were able to keep Janelle and Amy working without a break in services.

> And my God will meet all your needs according to the riches of his glory in Christ Jesus.
>
> Philippians 4:19

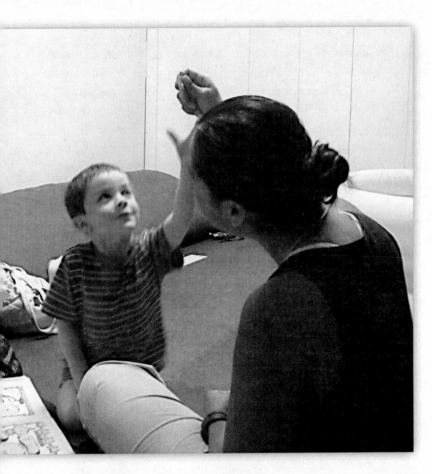

Season Fourteen

INTENSIVE EARLY
INTERVENTION

The next morning, we were back to our busy routine. The kids were up at seven, bathed, clothed, fed, brushed, and into the car, so I could get Devin to school by 8:15 a.m. I had to be back at the house for Ethan's first therapy session at 8:30. When we arrived home, Janelle was there waiting for us. Ethan and Janelle would work together for the next two hours, and then we were off to the play center from 11:00 a.m. to noon. We grabbed lunch before rushing home for his 1:00 p.m. appointment with Amy. Amy would spend two more hours with Ethan, and then we were off to pick up Devin from school.

After school, I would encourage the boys to play together. "But Mom," Devin would say, "Ethan is like a robot baby. He won't play with me, he just stares off into space; he doesn't even notice that I'm there. Do I have to play with him?" It broke my heart to hear Devin say such things, but I knew how he felt. I felt the same way.

"Devin," I'd respond, "Ethan learns differently than other kids, so we have to help teach him how to play with you, or he will never learn how to have friends."

It was hard on Devin, just like it would be for any child his age; he really wanted a brother to play with and talk to. What encouraged him was when I told him that he could be one of Ethan's best teachers.

Devin ended up becoming a big part of Ethan's escape from his world of autism. He would chase Ethan around the backyard and do whatever it took to get his brother to notice him and laugh at him. He taught Ethan how to ride his scooter around the basketball court. He pulled him around in the wagon and made Ethan tell him where he wanted to go. He pushed him on the swing set, and they jumped together on the trampoline. Ethan loved to have Devin bounce him as high as he could. He would laugh and say, "Again, again." It made me very happy to see my boys finally playing together.

At 5:30 p.m., Brian would arrive home, and we would all sit down for dinner. After dinner, Devin and Daddy would do homework, and I would take Ethan back to the therapy room where we would work on implementing all of the things that we worked on that day.

I wanted him to learn and absorb everything that we had been working on, so we could move on to the next goal. My flesh so badly wanted to take an early bath and cuddle up with Brian in front of the TV, but I knew that there was no time to waste. Ethan was my priority and how I felt did not matter. I wasn't going to leave one moment for autism to steal his thoughts.

Ethan and I would sit next to each other and read books, work with letters, sounds, and numbers. Then we would sit on the floor and roll a ball back and forth between us. As it got late, and he looked like he was getting tired, I would put him in his favorite blue spandex swing that we called the cocoon. I would swing him ever so softly and sing over him.

My lullabies were more than just soothing bedtime songs. I would sing songs filled with the Word of God that spoke of healing and restoration. As I sang I would visualize the areas of his mind that were undeveloped, and I would see them made whole in Jesus name.

At 8 p.m., we would put the boys in bed, pray with them, and then take the last couple of hours winding down from our hectic day.

Bedtime proved to be one of the best bonding times for the boys. Devin was very talkative. As they lay there in their beds, Devin would try to get Ethan to talk to him. At first, Ethan would not respond to direct questions, but he could repeat what was being said to him. I later learned that this is a condition called *echolalia*.

Devin learned how to use it to get his brother to respond to him. We would hear Devin teach Ethan to repeat words such as go, stop, Momma, Daddy, Auntie Kim, Papa, Grandpa, and Grandma. We wanted them to go right to sleep, but we allowed this to continue every night because we felt like it gave them valuable bonding time. It was through this bedtime ritual that they learned how to become friends and work together as brothers.

One night, we were blown away when we heard Devin teaching Ethan how to pray. "Ethan, say, Dear Jesus," he would respond, "Dear Jesus." Devin would continue, "Please bless Momma and Devin, and give us good dreams and heal Ethan, in Jesus name, Amen." Ethan wouldn't miss a beat; he was able to copy Devin's words exactly. As we listened, our eyes filled with tears of joy. We always prayed with them, but now they were praying by themselves. That was a great night to remember.

Ethan's third birthday had just passed. In celebration we met with our immediate family for a small birthday party. I would have loved to throw Ethan a big party, but I knew he would not respond to all the people, much less notice that the celebration was for him. I thought that we should wait and let him continue to develop a few more months. Devin's birthday was just two months away, so we planned on having a party for both of them at that time.

The party was on the last Saturday in June. We invited close to thirty adults and their children to come over for the celebration. We made it a superhero-themed birthday party. Papa rented a Spiderman jumper, a snow cone machine, and ten tables with chairs. We bought a Superman piñata and decorated the backyard with superhero balloons, tablecloths, and toys. My sister Kim even found a company that sends a real person dressed as superhero over to plays with the kids. We went all out!

Saturday soon arrived. Family and friends filled our house and backyard to capacity. Devin was very excited to have a party where all of the focus was on him. He and his friends ran around playing, shouting, and fighting each other with play swords.

He was in awe of the table of full of presents that were all for him. Ethan also had a table full of presents and lots of people wanting to hug him and say "happy birthday," but I could tell that he was starting to become overloaded. I don't think he could handle the noise and all of the excitement; he was definitely out of his comfort zone.

I looked on as all of the children ran around playing with each other but Ethan was not with them. As I looked for him, I found him in his therapy room all by himself, lying on his back, staring up at the ceiling fan.

My heart sank to see that he could not handle the sensory overload caused by the birthday crowd. What could I do? It was too late to cancel the party and tell everyone to go home.

I sat with him for a few minutes and then took him back outside. The first thing he did was run over to the balloons, rip them from the back of the chairs, and watch them fly off into the air. I ran over to stop him from destroying all of the decorations and decided to take him to the jumper and let him jump around with the other children.

Once inside, he started running into the other kids and knocking them over. Then he took the bouncy balls that we had in the jumper and threw them out onto the basketball court. He then proceeded to run over to a neatly stacked table full of presents, throwing each one to the ground.

I could see that getting Ethan to join in with all of the other children was not going to happen, so I took him back to his therapy room where he could find some peace and quiet.

This party was a big reminder of Ethan's condition. Some of my friends knew, and by the end of the day, I am sure that those who didn't could tell that something was wrong with him. It was becoming harder and harder for me to cover his behavior.

Because of the embarrassment and disappointment that I felt at the party, I started isolating myself from the general public. Most of my friends stopped calling and coming over. Because of Ethan's erratic behavior, I was no longer comfortable going out for normal errands.

I remember many times wishing that I could have my life back; I silently wished for the life I had before autism.

After many months, I realized I could not keep Ethan isolated forever. He was going to have to learn how to deal with people and with the circumstances of life, and I was going to have to endure the embarrassment until he figured it out.

Season Fifteen

Monday after the birthday party, Janelle and Amy both came with fresh ideas to help Ethan. They had seen a lot of his issues at the party and were ready to face them head on.

One of the many problems they saw was that Ethan would run right past, or over, anyone to get what he wanted. It was clear that we needed to include other children into Ethan's activities so he could learn to notice others and develop relationships.

Another problem they saw was what they referred to as hyper-focused. He would become so tuned in to what he was doing that he couldn't see anything else around him or notice any danger that may be coming his way. We needed to work with Ethan to help him open up to the world around him. We agreed that we had a lot of work ahead of us.

Over the next few weeks, we noticed that Ethan loved to learn. He was like a sponge that seemed to absorb everything with excitement. He loved discovering new things, so much so that he became obsessed with what we taught him.

One thing he loved was letters. All Ethan wanted us to do was to write them over and over again. Although he did not yet have the fine motor development to write, he had memorized the entire alphabet in upper and lower case letters. If we drew the letter incorrectly, he would act frustrated and cross it out, then he wanted us to start over from the beginning.

As the weeks progressed, he became fixated on the letter Z. It was his new favorite letter. As we walked through a parking lot Ethan's eyes would look at the license plates to find his this letter. He became so obsessed with it that if he did not see that letter at least once he would not want to get into the car. He would throw a fit and want to walk around the parking lot until he found the letter "Z". Because of the way he acted I feared someone would call the police or child protective services.

I decided to try to keep Ethan busy as we walked to and from the car so he wouldn't act out. I asked him questions such as, "What does a cat say? Where is your nose? Where is momma's eye? What is your favorite animal?" We would even sing the alphabet song or talk about his favorite book. I would try anything to keep him busy until we were in the car driving away.

Even though Ethan was making progress in many areas, I was still concerned about his issues, mood swings, and obsessive behaviors. Although he was learning and understanding letters and sounds, his obsession with the alphabet was worrying. I wondered how we could use this obsession to continue teaching him new things. His therapists and I came up with an idea.

When Ethan wanted us to write down a particular letter, for example the letter A, we would first ask him to tell us the name of something that started with that letter. "Apple," he would respond. Then we would draw an apple and the letter A. We continued to do this with every letter, and eventually we were able to get his mind off letters and sounds and on to words and there meanings.

During his therapy sessions, Ethan was still drawn to the letter activities. To help him break his obsession, we implemented a written schedule into his class times. If Ethan had a one-hour session, they would split the time into six, ten-minute activities. On a white board, they would write out each activity, always putting his favorite letter activity in the last position.

To fill in the other activities, they would give Ethan a list of choices, and they would take turns picking the activities for the session. This helped teach Ethan how to work with other people and also to take turns. In addition, it showed him that he would be rewarded at the end with his favorite game if he completed all of his assignments.

Over the next few weeks, we invited friends of the family over to join him in his sessions. When his brother was home from school, he would also join in. All of these people came around to help Ethan learn how to work in different social situations and how to relate with different people.

As time progressed, we could see how smart Ethan was becoming. One day while at the Play Center, Ethan was asked to make a caterpillar out of play dough. His therapist demonstrated it to him by rolling small balls and putting them together to form a caterpillar. But Ethan took all the balls of play dough and formed them into one large ball then set it down and said, "Cocoon." It became clear that a very intelligent person was locked up inside of Ethan's body.

In another session, his therapist asked him to draw a stick figure of himself. As he drew it, she asked, "Aren't you going to put some clothes on?" Ethan then drew a box around the figure with water drops falling from the wall and said, "Shower!" I was tickled to see my Italian humor coming out of him.

Season Sixteen

DEFEAT AUTISM NOW

A few months earlier, we had taken Ethan to a D.A.N. (Defeat Autism Now) doctor. D.A.N. is a group of doctors, scientists, and research teams who have committed their careers to finding the cause and cure for autism. I had never heard of this group of doctors until I came across a web site called TACA. (www.tacanow.com)

Talk About Curing Autism was started by the mother of an autistic child who wanted to bring everyone together to talk about what was working with their children. On that website was a page that talked about professionals who look at the medical side of this mental disorder.

I wondered if there could be something medically wrong in Ethan's body that may be causing some of his symptoms. I was not sure but I had to look into every possible explanation to see if I could find an answer.

One of the many things that D.A.N doctors do is test for food allergies to see if a food or protein in that food may be causing an adverse reaction in the body. They also perform tests that look for intestinal bacteria, yeast overgrowth, and/or accumulation of heavy metals. The presence of any of these can cause a negative reaction in the body and produce erratic behavior in the child.

Since we had already seen the benefit of removing wheat and dairy from Ethan's diet, we thought that we should further explore their other recommendations. The next step according to the D.A.N protocol was to have a broad panel of tests done to see what other issues may be going on.

With a little research, we found Dr. Winn. He is a board certified pediatrician and D.A.N doctor. To our pleasant surprise, not only was he a pediatrician, he was also the father of an autistic child.

We learned a lot that afternoon about the medical side of autism, and we left with a handful of blood and urine tests for Ethan to complete. We drew blood for a food allergy test; we cut of a small section off his hair for a heavy metals test, and we collected tubes of urine and fecal matter to test for intestinal bacteria and yeast overgrowth.

Since these tests were not deemed medically necessary by the insurance company, we had to pay for them out of our pocket. We did not have the money to spend on these tests but we felt compelled to do so nonetheless. What choice did we really have? We had to do everything in our power to help our son. We ended up putting most of the cost on our credit cards.

The results of the tests were not encouraging. On paper, Ethan looked like a mess. He was allergic to many of the foods we were feeding him. We came to find out that Ethan had twenty food allergies! While we thought we were helping him by substituting cow's milk with almond milk, he was in fact allergic to almonds as well.

To top it all off, he was also allergic to some of his favorite fruits. He could no longer eat bananas, cantaloupe, oranges or have any more nuts. In addition to these, he was also allergic to oats, rice, wheat, eggs, sesame seeds and certain oils. We immediately removed these foods from his diet.

His hair test showed that Ethan had very high levels of aluminum, cadmium, lead, silver, tin, titanium, mercury, and arsenic in his body. Brian said to me, "How can this be? How is it possible that a three year old is overloaded with these toxins? What is going on? Could arsenic kill our baby? Are these metals causing our son to act autistic? Have they caused the delay in his speech and social development?"

A third set of tests soon arrived and the results revealed that Ethan had very high levels of yeast and fungal overgrowth. I asked myself, *Is this like a yeast infection?* I wondered what his little stomach must feel like. No wonder he was irritable and crabby. Maybe this is why his skin is so dry and his eyes foggy, red, and discolored. I wondered if these problems were responsible for the patchy areas of eczema that kept coming back.

His doctor was not surprised to see these results. He said that most of the children that have autism had very similar test results. He then explained the results to us, telling us that arsenic is present in the pesticides that are used on foods that we eat and anything grown out of the soil may deposit these and other metals into our bodies.

Aluminum and mercury have been used as preservatives in vaccines for decades. Some children do not have the ability to flush these toxins out of their bodies like other children.

My question to the doctor was, "What do we do to fix all of these problems in Ethan's body?" One by one, he began making specific recommendations.

First, he told us about the importance of organic fruits, vegetables, and meats. Even with these, he said, "It is critically important to wash everything before you eat it." He continued to tell us that as we removed the foods he's allergic to, Ethan's stomach or gut would start to heal itself. "As the stomach issues heal, we might see the allergies drop off one by one and maybe even completely."

To deal with the yeast and fungal overgrowth, we would have to put Ethan on a yeast medication called Nystatin® and supplement high amounts of probiotics. We would then have to avoid foods that could cause the yeast to flare up and continue to use the probiotics to keep healthy yeast levels in his body.

As for the high amount of metals, we had to make a choice. We could either put him through a process called *chelation* or we could use high amounts of vitamins and minerals and wait to see if his body would start to cleanse itself. We chose to go with the supplements and hope and pray that his body would repair itself. In time, we found that this new approach to cleansing the body and changing his diet proved to be very beneficial.

With the new diet, vitamin supplements, yeast medication, and intensive early-intervention, we felt like we were doing all we could do. Every week, we had eighteen hours of in-home therapy, two hours at the Play Center, and two hours at the Center for Speech and Language Pathology. Through it all we continued to pray and believe for his healing. We were doing everything that God had led us to do. Although we did not know how all of this was going to lead to Ethan's healing, we continued to believe that God did.

Within weeks of changing Ethan's diet, and dealing with his yeast problems, we saw Ethan become a new child. His skin cleared up, his irritability went down, his speech continued to improve, he stopped rubbing his body against the walls, and he started recognizing more words.

Ethan continued to make progress in every area, but he still had a lot of work to do. He was showing exceptional growth in his expressive and receptive language and in his academics, but he still could not button his own pants, get to the toilet on time, or hold a conversation with a friend. We just weren't seeing much development in social behavior. He would much rather be watching television, or playing by himself, instead of spending time with his brother or family.

We continued to work hard to help Ethan in any way we could, but the enormous cost of it all drove us into debt. I remember Brian and I sitting down one night to discuss how much we had spent on doctor visits, medical tests, and therapies. Brian explained that our medical insurance only covered twenty therapies per year, and we were very close to reaching our limit. Without insurance, we would soon have to absorb the cost of almost a thousand dollars a month just for the Floortime Play Center.

Clearly, we did not have the money to pay these bills, but for me, there was no other choice. I knew that God had given me a word and showed me that Ethan would be well by the age of five, but I could not stand by and wait for that day to come, I had to stay busy. I knew that "Faith without works is dead," (James 2:20-26) so I had to keep working, and trust that if God opens a door, He would provide a way to walk through it.

I told Brian, "I don't care if I have to sell my clothes and all my shoes; we have to find a way to make this work. I really don't care if we lose the house. Our kids are more important than our stuff." It was at that point that Brian and I decided that we would not be governed by our finances. We would do whatever God led us to do. We would trust in Him and not trust in our feelings or emotions.

Before long, our insurance had reached its limit. We were now faced with paying out of pocket to cover the costs of Ethan's therapy. When my dad learned about our predicament, He was gracious enough to cover all of costs until we could change to an insurance plan that offered unlimited behavioral health.

OUR FIRST CONVERSATION

One day I put Ethan down for a nap before his afternoon session. As usual, I leaned over, gave him a kiss, and told him that I loved him. Normally he would lay there and script a scene from *Dora the Explorer* or recite the letters and sounds of the alphabet, but on this day I could tell that something was different. His eyes were clear, and he wasn't staring off into space. He seemed to be paying attention to me, so I decided to stay for a moment longer. As I lay down beside him, I asked, "Are you ready to take a little rest?"

In response he answered, "No, I'll just lay with Momma for a little bit." He turned his body toward me and looked right in my eyes. They were so clear—so beautiful; it was as if I was looking into them for the very first time.

"I love you Ethan."

I heard for the first time, "I love you too, Momma." Tears ran down my face as my son and I had our first conversation. We talked back and forth for four or five minutes. Then I kissed him and left him to rest.

I could not believe what just happened. I went to my room, thanked God, and cried tears of joy. I wanted to call and tell everyone I knew. First I called Brian, and then my sister and a few of my closest friends. We were all overjoyed by the astonishing progress that Ethan had made. As I hung up the phone, I thanked God that all of the hard work, the long hours, the money spent, and the tears cried, had finally paid off.

I'VE GOT JOY

You've turned my mourning into dancing
You have given me new joy
My heart will sing and not be silent
I will shout your praises Lord

I will bless you Lord forever
For you came and rescued me
I will praise you Lord my savior
You're the reason why I sing

I've got the joy, joy, joy, joy,
    down in my heart
The joy, joy, joy, joy, down in my heart
Joy, joy, joy, joy, down in my heart
Down in my heart to stay

Peace like a river flowing through my soul
Love overwhelming cause
    You are in control
Peace like a river flowing through my soul
Love overwhelming I rejoice
    because I know

Season Seventeen

TRANSITIONING TO SCHOOL

Just before Ethan turned four years old we received a date for a new IEP. The school district was hoping that he would now be ready to transition to public education.

Once again, we set up appointments with the psychologist, the school nurse, the occupational therapist, and the speech and language pathologist. The new assessments showed that Ethan was very bright and loved to learn, but he was still far behind his age group in many areas.

The school's multidisciplinary assessment showed that Ethan's cognitive and academic skills ranged from age appropriate to five-and-a-half years of age. His fine motor, gross motor, as well as his social/emotional skills, were all age appropriate. The areas of concern seemed to be his self-help skills. In toileting, feeding, and dressing, Ethan had only developed to the level of a twenty-three-month-old. Other problem behaviors included a lack of extended focus during activities, wandering off, over-reacting and throwing tantrums.

We had our own assessments done like we did at the first IEP, and we could see the amazing progress that he made in the last eighteen months. His first test on October 12, 2006, showed that although his motor skills were developing normally, he showed delay in social and emotional development. He only understood and expressed language like a one year old.

Now just eighteen months later, Ethan had shown improvement in every area. His cognition development (attention, remembering, producing and understanding language, solving problems, and making decisions) now proved to be at three and a half to four years of age, and his language, once his weakest area, now proved to be his strongest at four to five years of age. And his social/emotional development was improving but still not yet age appropriate.

We knew about his continued delays, but also knew how far he had come. We were not going to sit back and let him be placed somewhere that would stop his forward progress. We only wanted what was best for him, and we were not going to settle for anything less.

The IEP went as we expected. The school district wanted to transition Ethan into the preschool class that they had developed. It was a special day class for the developmentally challenged. The only pupils would be other disabled children. During the week, they said that a speech and occupational therapist would each spend thirty minutes with the class as a whole to help them grow in their development.

We appreciated the services that they had developed for these children, but we knew that they were not right for our son. Ethan was making too much progress. We felt that including him in such a classroom would hurt his development. We saw the importance of a school program and the need for a structured class with children his age, but we also knew that if he was going to learn and excel, he needed to be around non-disabled peers.

Once again, we were at odds with the school district. They wanted to include Ethan in what they had established, but we wanted to give him the best preparation for a normal and successful future. We knew that if we worked slowly and taught Ethan how to interact and operate in a regular classroom environment, he could do it, and by kindergarten we could reach our goal of enrolling him in a non-disabled classroom.

We knew that it was time to call our attorney. A phone call later, we found out that he had moved to another state. "What are we to do now?" I asked. "Who else can we call, and how much is it going to cost us to fight the school district?"

Over the next few days, we called friends, other parents of children with autism, and special education law offices, all in search to find the right lawyer who was willing to take our case. Some friends told us about an attorney who had a lot of success with the school districts in our area. Our excitement quickly turned to frustration when we learned that the initial consultation was six hundred dollars.

How would we pay for this? There was absolutely no way we could afford it. We already spent all we had on special foods, supplements, therapies, and medical insurance. Desperate, we turned to God. We prayed for guidance, and we trusted Him to lead us to the right attorney and provide the way to cover all the costs.

After many calls, God led us to Mr. Lee. He answered his own phone and seemed to be very knowledgeable in the field of special education law. As I explained Ethan's diagnosis and how far he had come, he was silent and seemed shocked. I assumed by his silence that he had many questions. Maybe he thought, *"Are these parents really telling the truth, or are they blinded by the love for their child?"* Although he didn't ask them, I could tell that he was hesitant to believe my story. But by the end of our conversation, he had loosened up and told me that he would love to come and hear more, see the IEP paperwork, and meet our son.

I had a feeling that we had found the right man; anyone who would drive forty-five miles to come and hear our story and meet our son had to be a lawyer with a heart. I didn't talk about money or ask about his consultation fee because it really didn't matter to me. We had decided to give it to God and let Him work it out.

Mr. Lee showed up right on time. He stepped out of his BMW, paused for moment, grabbed his briefcase, and walked to our front door. He was a well-dressed, young Asian man who looked like he had just graduated from law school.

Brian and I looked at each other and thought the same thing, *He's so young. Does he have the experience to fight the school district and get Ethan what he needs?* Soon, our fears were calmed as we realized that right in front of us was another angel sent from heaven to walk us through the next season of our journey.

After reviewing Ethan's IEP and reading all his charts, Mr. Lee told us that it looked like we had a good case.

He then asked to meet Ethan. We called Ethan in and told him to say "hi." We had Ethan tell him about his favorite animals and games. Ethan asked him his name and then he ran back to finish a puzzle he had started. We could see that Mr. Lee was impressed when he asked, "Is this the same kid in this paper work?" He then excused himself and went outside to make a phone call.

When he returned, he said, "I don't take cases that I don't think I can win, but this looks like a good case, and I am going to help you. The only thing I ask is that you let me do all of the talking with the school district from this point on, and you do everything that I ask you to do. Don't make any moves or decision about this case unless you talk to me."

Brian and I looked at each other and I thought, *Are you serious? This is awesome.* In my mind I said, *Praise God!* But I know Brian was still worried about how much this was going to cost us.

Mr. Lee continued and said, "To take on this case I have to charge you a retainer fee, however I see so much potential in Ethan's case that I'm only going to charge you one dollar."

One dollar—is this a joke? Who charges one dollar?

He went on to say, "In the end, when we win this case, I will submit my bill to the school district and once they pay the bill, I will mail you back your dollar."

This was incredible! We never thought that we could get an attorney to fight the school district and in the end make the school district pay the bill.

Mr. Lee then sent a letter of representation to the school district as well as to the State Board of Education. He drafted a formal complaint detailing why Ethan should not be included in a special day class, but instead, continue in home therapy. He concluded by asking the school board to accept his request for due process.

Soon, we had another letter from the state with a big bold inscription across the top that said: "Ethan Walden versus the School District."

In preparation for our trial, our lawyer advised us to get our own assessment from a child psychologist. He said "If we end up in court, I can use this outside assessment to counter the school districts assessment." This was the only cost that we had to incur, and it was well worth the six hundred dollars.

The child psychologist came to our house and spent many hours with Ethan. As he looked over Ethan's test results from the Regional Center, he saw they showed an Autism Index score of 102 (Probability of Autism– Very Likely) and an Autism Diagnostic score of 18. He explained to us that the higher the score the more severe the autism.

The doctor then took time to retest him and obtain an up to date analysis of his developmental levels. These results showed an IQ score of 110, a picture vocabulary score of an 8-9 year old, a letter-word identification score of 7-9 year old, a comprehension age score of 6-9 year old, and finally an Autism Diagnostic score of 13.

We could see that Ethan was making progress at home, but seeing it on paper was very encouraging. "Praise God," I said, "Ethan's autism is leaving just as God showed me."

The doctor's report continued, "Ethan is already showing a variety of academic strengths. He has largely taught himself not only to read sentences and short pas- sages, but short passages for comprehension. Both of these tasks score at a very superior level, corresponding to the 99th percentile."

In conclusion, the doctor wrote:

> Ethan is a very intelligent boy, with a variety of skills many years beyond his actual age level. Many academic tasks are at the second grade level and putting him in a special education class with students below grade level would likely interfere with his ability to learn at the level at which he is capable. In my recommendation, Ethan should be placed in a general education class with a behaviorally trained aid to help him succeed in a structured education program.

Brian and I looking over this assessment and knew what we needed to do. We were to immediately enroll him in a regular preschool class and send one of his therapists in to shadow him and teach him how to learn in a group setting.

After looking at many preschools in the area, we found the right fit with our own church family. The Rock Church had just started their own preschool, and they were more than willing to help Ethan integrate into a structured education program.

Season Eighteen

PRESCHOOL

As his first day of preschool quickly approached, Ethan and I went shopping for his first backpack. We filled his backpack with pencils, crayons, paper, scissors, erasers, and a folder in preparation for the big day.

Ethan was ready for his first day of preschool, but I don't think I was. This transition was particularly hard for me. I had nursed him, fed him, and loved and protected him since birth. Ethan and I have learned a lot together, and I had dedicated twenty-four hours a day seven days a week, pulling him from his world into ours. Now I had to let him go and trust someone else to watch over him, love him, and look out for his best interest.

When my fears did rise up in me, I'd say, "God has not given me a spirit of fear, but of a sound mind, so I will trust in Him."

Once at school, when issues and problems did arise, Ethan's aid would carefully document the behaviors so all of his therapists could address them at home and find tools to help Ethan overcome them. At home, they would develop "social stories" to help him understand the appropriate response to the different situations he faced.

A social story is a simple description of an everyday social interaction written from a child's perspective. Social stories can be used in different situations. We used them to prepare Ethan for upcoming changes in routine and to learn the appropriate response during classroom and playground activities. We felt that if Ethan could rehearse the story ahead of time, then he had would have an idea and a picture in his head as to how to act the next time that situation occurred.

At school during reading time, the children would gather into a circle as the teacher read them a story. Ethan wanted to crawl up in her lap, so he could read along and look at the pictures with her, just like he did with me at home.

Why should it be any different here? he must have wondered. While other children could learn by watching and following the teacher's instructions, Ethan couldn't. He had to be taught each rule individually and sometimes over and over again until he got it.

Another problem he had was spacial awareness. He would sit so close to another child that he would almost be sitting in their lap. If he wanted to speak to them, he would get right in their face. At play time when he ran to join in with others, he would not stop in time and would usually run into them.

As issues came up in school, Amy and Janelle would create incomplete stories of children playing together. They would then ask Ethan to help complete the story so everyone ended up being friends. Our goal was to help him understand that other children had feelings too. If we took something from them, their feelings would be hurt, but if we played with them and shared with them, they would be happy.

To help teach Ethan space awareness, his therapists came up with a game called *Space Invaders*. We would walk in a line, and whenever one of us would get too close to the other person, we would have Ethan yell out, "Space invader."

Over and over again, we practiced skits to help model the correct behavior. It took a couple months but Ethan soon caught on and was able to correct his issue with personal space.

One thing that helped Ethan recognize and care for others was when we taught him to read facial expressions.

We bought books that depicted the feelings of other people in picture form. As we looked at them, I would ask Ethan to tell me how they felt.

"Ethan, do they look happy, sad or angry? It looks like this boy is sad because his friend is not sharing with him. What do you think?" As we talked about other people's feelings, Ethan learned to look at the expressions of other people and try to figure out how they felt.

As we identified Ethan's issues and came up with ways to deal with them, we saw marked improvements. Some things were harder than others, but with time, patience, and prayer, we always saw Ethan improve. After hard days, I would remind him that every day was a new opportunity to try and make it better than the day before.

On the way to school I would tell him, "Ethan, today is a brand new day. Even though you had a few problems yesterday, you can turn it around, and today can be a positive day." I reminded him that mommy and daddy believed in him, and God believed in him. I told him, "I know you can do it. Today is going to be a great day."

As his behavior improved, Ethan was asked on many occasions to come up and read a book for the class. To everyone's amazement, this pre-k student could not only read, he even knew how to put emotion into the characters of the story. The children where surprised that someone their age could read. The adults were impressed that he had the ability, at such a young age, to differentiate between the characters of the story.

The improvements that we saw as we walked through this journey were astounding. We could see that God's hand was truly on Ethan.

Meanwhile, our court date was fast approaching. A week before the trial date, we had the opportunity to meet with the head of the special education department and try to come to an agreement.

Mr. Lee met us outside where we went over our case one last time. Once inside we sat down in the same office we had been in a few months back. This time sitting across from us was a school district lawyer as well as the head of special education. They started by highly recommending their special education class for Ethan and tried to convince us of its benefits.

Mr. Lee then carefully laid out our case. He explained that Ethan had started a pre-school class at the Kids Rock Learning Center. "During the last three months", he said "Ethan has shown remarkable progress not only in his ability to learn, but also in his ability to become a contribution to the class. Ethan has made friends, encouraged others, helped with classroom chores, and learned how to become a part of a group." He then presented written recommendations from his classroom aid and pre-school teacher.

About an hour went by as both sides presented their case. By the end of it all, Mr. Lee was able to show that Ethan could not only fit in with a regular education classroom, but with a personal aid, he could flourish.

The Director then asked us to excuse her as she and the district lawyer went to speak in private. When they returned they gave us the news that we had been waiting to hear. They agreed with our position and gave us everything we asked for.

That day, we saw what would have been our attorney bill of $7,500 vanish. Just as he said many months before as we sat around our kitchen table. "If we can prove and win Ethan's case, the school district will be required to pay for my services." Brian and I were both amazed that God had, once again, worked all things out for good.

About two weeks later we received a letter in the mail from our attorney which congratulated us on the outcome of our case. Attached to that letter was a bill for his services. It was clearly stamped "Paid in Full." Neatly folded in between the two pages was also a crisp one- dollar bill. Just as he promised he mailed us back our dollar.

> Being confident of this, that he who began a good work in you will carry it on to completion until the day of Christ Jesus.
>
> Philippians 1:6

Season Nineteen

As part of the agreement, we could pick any school in the district, and they would train an aid to shadow Ethan in a regular kindergarten class.

Although the start of the new school year was still six months away, I wanted to find the right placement for Ethan. Who would be the best teacher? Who would be patient with Ethan's growth and see his potential instead of his deficits? What school principal would give Ethan the needed support and see his true potential? I knew that God had the right fit and that He would lead me to the right place. I just had to go and find it.

I went online and looked up every elementary school in the district. I looked at the performance of each school and picked out over a dozen schools that Brian and I decided to visit.

I made appointments with every one of the principals and met each of the kindergarten teachers. Initially, they were kind, professional, and excited to see that a parent was actually interested in their child's education. It was not until they learned of Ethan's diagnosis that their demeanor changed. It's not that they were rude; I just don't think they wanted to deal with a child that had autistic behaviors, and I'm sure they had enough difficulties in their classrooms already. Each principal reminded me that the school district had created classes for these children, and I should give them a try.

Within a couple weeks, I had reached the bottom of my list of schools. There was only one school left. It had only been open a couple years, and it was located in a brand new development.

The school was gorgeous; the playground was huge; the buildings were large and bright, loaded with brand new computers, books, and desks. It had the best of everything. When I checked on the best schools in the area, this school was rated #1. If it was up to me, I wanted Ethan there. I couldn't wait to meet the teachers and the principal and sign Ethan up for his first year of kindergarten.

I walked into her office and could tell that she ran a very structured school. She looked like she loved what she was doing. By the awards on the wall, I could see that she was very proud of her students and teachers.

I introduced myself and told her that I was looking for the best school to enroll my son in. It wasn't long before I told her about his diagnosis. She was taken aback. I think, like the previous principals, she thought that I was ignorant and unrealistic about his condition.

Even without meeting him, she concluded that her school would not be the best place for Ethan. Like everyone else, she recommended that he should be placed in the class that had been created for children with autistic disorders.

I assured her that Ethan was ready for a mainstream class. Her response was, "I cannot deny you placement here, but I strongly encourage you to enroll him in a class that has been designed to meet the needs of these children." I took that as a closed door and knew that this was not going to be the right fit either.

On the ride home, I was discouraged. My sister was with me that day, and she saw my frustration. "Everything is going to work out," she said. "God is one your side, and He knows the right place for Ethan." I could always count on my sister. Since my mom died, she had become my closest friend, and she always knew what to say to encourage me and build me up.

I called Brian and told him that I couldn't find one school that was right for Ethan. "Are you sure you checked every school?" he asked.

"Yes, I checked every school on my list. There is one that might work, but I really don't feel a peace about any of them."

I was feeling very discouraged. We had worked so hard and come so far, and now all I saw were closed doors. I asked God what I should do, and I prayed that He would show me the right school to enroll Ethan in.

I remembered Philippians 1:6, "Being confident of this, that he who began a good work in you will carry it out to completion until the day of Christ Jesus."

As I recited this verse in my mind, I heard God speak to me and say, "Keep pressing forward, run the race and you will finish the course with joy."

I WILL RUN

Some mistake this marathon,
For the race that's quickly gone
It's in Christ I carry on
I'm determined to finish strong
Some mistake these tear filled eyes
For one believing lies
Persevering never dies
When hope will bring a another try

I will run, I'll overcome
I'm holding on, new days have just begun
And by your grace, I'll run this race.
Until the day, I've finished and I've won!

I've been praying at 3 am,
He restores my faith again
Just a human made in flesh
Sleep deprived He is my rest
There is no other choice
I'm listening for His voice
I'm desperate for His strength
Advancing till I see His Face

I will run, I'll overcome
I'm holding on, new days have just begun
And by your grace, I'll run this race.
Until the day, I've finished and I've won!

He changed me through adversity
Made stronger in the suffering
Believing what He said
Pressing toward the road ahead

The cutoff date to enroll Ethan in kindergarten was fast approaching. I wanted to wait to officially enroll him until I found the right school. With time running out, I knew I had to make a decision immediately. Even though I had not yet picked a school the district told me to sign him up now and file transfer papers when I found the right placement for him.

As I walked into the registration office, I had an empty feeling in my stomach. It was time to officially open the next season of Ethan's life.

As I approached the front desk, my eyes caught an inscription on a plaque sitting on top of the desk. It read: "The will of God will never take you where the Grace of God will not protect you."

That was for me. As I read it, God's peace came over me. I was reminded that He was with me and that he would lead me to the right place.

That night, Brian and I went over the list of schools again. Maybe, we'd missed something. Curiously, there was one school that we assumed was in a different district. Well, it turned out we were wrong. It was in our district. A little flame of excitement began to grow. *Was God giving us one more opportunity, one more possibility for Ethan?*

The next morning, my sister picked me up, and we drove over to the school to see if this was indeed the place God had for us. I quietly wondered if this was this the right school, with the right teacher, and the right principal.

As we pulled in, we saw an old, small school that was not in the best area of town. Many of the buildings were different colors, the playground was tiny, and it was next to a fairly busy street. I thought to myself, *Oh no, this couldn't be the one!* As I walked onto the campus, a peace came over me and a quiet voice inside me said, "*This is it, this is the one.*"

A voice spoke up from behind us "Good morning, can I help you?". A well-dressed lady was walking toward us. I thought to myself, *Gina, do not waste any time like you did at the other schools. Just get right to the point.*

I said, "Hi, my name is Gina and my son is going to be starting kindergarten next year. My sister and I have come to tour the school and see if this might be the right place to put him."

In response I heard, "Thanks for coming by. I'd love to show you around."

I started right away saying, "My son's name is Ethan, and he has a diagnosis of autism. A couple years ago he could not speak. He would not respond to my voice, and he would just sit there and stare off into space. He was in really bad shape."

"Wow," she stated, "I'm sorry to hear that." I continued to tell her that through a lot of work, Ethan was now a different child. "My husband and I have had him in twenty-five hours of weekly intervention, and through the hard work of many great people, he can now talk and interact with others. Today, he's not only in a regular preschool class, he's the smartest kid there."

She responded, "That's incredible. I have a friend with a child on the spectrum, so I know how hard it can be. It sounds like you've done a great job."

I proceeded to tell her, "I recently received permission from the school district to put Ethan in a regular kindergarten class, so I am hoping that this might be the right school for him."

I was a little nervous, so I probably gave her more information than she needed, but to my surprise, she seemed to be impressed by everything I told her. Her response was very different from all the others. She said, "I'm not the principal of the school, but I think you found the right place. I'm sure that Ethan would fit in here just fine. I would love for you to meet our principal, but he is not in the office today. I'll tell him about you and have him call you in the morning."

A sense of calm came over me—a peace and joy that I had not found since I started looking at the many options for Ethan's first year of public education. I was thankful as God was clearly opening a new door and revealing the next step for our family.

Next, she introduced us to the kindergarten teacher. She too did not seem concerned at all about his diagnosis. In fact, she told me to bring him back the next day to meet her.

As promised, the principal called me first thing the next morning. I told him about all the work that we had put into Ethan over the past few years. He was excited to hear of his progress and did not have one problem with Ethan coming to his school. He too said he was looking forward to meeting Ethan and told me to bring him in after lunch, so we could show him around.

When we walked onto the campus, Ethan wanted to know which room the kindergarten class would be in. "Well Ethan, I met your new teacher yesterday, she is a very nice lady, would you like to go meet her?"

"Let's go," he said.

I led him to her classroom and introduced him to the lady that would soon be his Kindergarten teacher.

He looked at all of the posters and pictures on the walls, and after a few moments, turned to the teacher and said, "Where are all the kids?" Before she could answer he continued, "I like your calendar. Look…January, February, March, April…Did you know that Valentine's Day is in February? My birthday is in May. It is on May 19. When is your birthday?"

I think she was a little stunned as she turned and looked at me with a surprised look on her face. In response, I just smiled.

Turning back toward him, she explained that kindergarten class starts at eight thirty in the morning and the children go home at twelve thirty.

Ethan looked at the clock and responded, "It's one fifteen. That means everyone already went home? I hope the kids had a great day."

"He's very chatty, isn't he?" She was amazed at all his questions.

I let Ethan look around the classroom and read a couple books as the teacher and I talked. She was very impressed with how much he knew. At one point she said to me, "He has autism? You would never know it. Can you tell me what you guys have done to get him this far?"

Next, it was time to meet the principal. As Ethan walked in his office, the principal got down on one knee to meet him. I could tell just by watching that this man knew how to really connect with a child. He knew his six-foot frame may be intimidating to Ethan, so he came down to his level and talked with him like he was a member of his own family. He said, "Hi Ethan, I am Mr. D. Would you like to come to our school? We would love to have you!"

Ethan replied with a simple, "Sure." Mr. D then gave him a high five, led him out of the office, and showed him around the campus.

Ethan was eager to start kindergarten right away, but the beginning of the school year was still a few months away so he agreed to finish the rest of the school year at the Kids Rock Learning Center. There we continued to work with him to overcome any issues that would keep him from being successful in a school environment.

One of those issues had to do with losing. Ethan hated to lose. Whatever game he was playing, if he didn't win he would throw himself on the ground and have a tantrum.

One day out on the playground, the class was participating in team races. Ethan took off hoping to win, but when he realized he was behind the other runner; he turned and ran in the other direction. He would do anything to avoid having to accept the fact that he lost.

At home with the help of his therapists, we acted out scenarios that showed Ethan how silly his actions were. I would purposefully lose or make a mistake and start crying dramatically throwing myself on the ground. One of his therapists would then ask, "Ethan, is Mommy acting the right way? What do you think she should do?" In doing this, we helped him see that this type of behavior was not correct, and we gave him a chance to come up with an alternative response.

As we gave him a chance to figure out how to regulate his own behavior, he soon was able to suggest the correct responses. With time and a lot of effort, he learned that it was better to stay and deal with the problem instead of run away from it.

To help regulate Ethan's outbursts, his teachers at the Play Center came up with a great idea. They taught him about the scale system. They showed Ethan a scale and told him that a small, insignificant problem was a level one problem. A really big one was a level ten problem.

When he threw a tantrum over something small like cutting outside a dotted line, we would say, "Excuse me, Ethan, is that a number ten problem? I think that's a number one problem. Maybe we should just ask for another paper and try again. What do you think?"

We also used the scale system to help him control his volume level. He had problems keeping his volume at the proper level; especially when he was excited.

We knew he understood the scale system. I think he could see a picture in his head of a hand going up and down a scale, stopping at the appropriate level. If he was speaking too loud, we would tell him that he needed to lower his speaking level from eight to three. Immediately, he would bring his voice down. Eventually he got it, it's not to say that he didn't raise it again, but with practice, he learned to control his volume.

August of that year was soon upon us, and it was time for Ethan to start kindergarten. Since it was still summer, I bought him shorts and t-shirts, and two new pairs of tennis shoes. For his first day of school, Ethan wanted the latest Super Mario® backpack and all of the matching folders that go with it.

Monday morning I had him pose for pictures so we could remember his first day of kindergarten. Then we were off to school. Ethan was very excited to meet his new classmates and sit in his new desk.

As he walked in he said, "Hi, everyone," then he walked around the desks looking for his seat. I watched as he found his name on his assigned desk, then ran to the wall and hung up his backpack. He grabbed a book, like the teacher had asked, and returned to his seat right across from the cutest little girl, who promptly said "Hi."

Ethan looked up from his book, read her name, and replied, "Your name is Gracie. I'm Ethan! Do you want to look at my book?" I was so proud, my "little man" was making a new friend.

As I was getting ready to leave Ethan to his new class, he ran over and gave me a big hug. "I did it, Mom, I'm a kindergartner. You can go home now. I'll see you at twelve thirty. Bye."

I was so excited for him. Seeing Ethan start kindergarten with non-disabled children was something I had dreamed about for the last three years.

I could tell that Ethan's new friend Gracie was very shy. She didn't seem comfortable with the other kids in class, but she had a special connection with Ethan. Later that day, his aide told me they spent most of the day together. During lunch and recess, they even walked around holding hands.

That entire year went by with very few issues. Ethan quickly learned everyone's name, and made lots of friends. He loved his teacher, and he loved going to school. Every day as I dropped him off, he would run across the parking lot and give Gracie the biggest hug, and then they would walk to class together. I was in awe as I watched my son, who contrary to the educated opinions of medical doctors and developmental experts, become the most popular kid in class.

The only issue we did have was Ethan becoming bored, and disrupting the class. We saw that the problem would present itself during long periods of seat work.

He would finish his work so fast that he would end up talking and playing around, which caused disruptions in class. To keep him busy, his IEP team developed what we called a "Busy Folder."

When he was done with his required classroom work, his aide would pull out additional work for him and let him work on more challenging first-grade curriculum. This seemed to do the trick and keep Ethan occupied until it was time for the next activity.

Many mornings, I would stand in the back of the class-room and quietly watch as Ethan sat in class. One morning, God reminded me of a vision He had given me a couple of years before. It was an exactly picture of what I was seeing right in front of me. With tears in my eyes, I could see that He had fulfilled every promise He had given me.

It had all been worth it; every tear I cried; every battle we fought; every sleepless night; every exhausting day; every frantic run from one therapy session to the next … It had all been worth it!

Later that year, we went back to see Dr. Winn. This time we were not there for treatment; we just wanted to show the doctor who Ethan had become. Ethan walked in, and right away noticed the laptop on his desk. He asked, "Do you have any games on there? I like playing Super Mario Brothers. Do you like Super Mario?" He went on to tell him about his school, his friends, and his best friend Gracie.

Dr. Winn's eyes widened as he turned toward us and said, "I can't believe this is the same child." He then checked Ethan's heartbeat, blood pressure, and all the other things doctors do giving him a clean bill of health. Then he looked up at me and Brian saying, "I want to congratulate you. I believe that God really is healing your child."

Driving home that night, I began to see why God allowed us to walk through this trial. He wanted us to go through this so we could give hope to those facing a hopeless diagnosis. I believe that God put this story together because He knew one day you would be reading this and need to hear this testimony at this time in your life.

What hopeless situation are you facing? What diagnosis have you been given? Have you given up hope? No matter what may lie ahead, the same amazing grace that brought us through is available to you. There is nothing too hard for our God. In fact, we know that with God, nothing is impossible to those who believe. He really is the God of the impossible.

I encourage you to reach for God and hold onto His promises. Know that He is faithful to fulfill His plans for you. Remember that He fashioned you in your mother's womb and made you for such a time as this. He has written the storybook of your life and knows it from beginning to end. He has a plan and a purpose for your life, so don't give up! Lift your eyes to the hills and soon your brand new day will come.

STORYBOOK

He knows me, He loves me
He hears the thoughts I'm thinking
He sees inside my dreams
He formed this Heart that's beating
He has a plan for me,
    beyond my understanding
He holds my destiny,
    so I stand firm believing

He has written the story book of my life
He knows my morning until night
Now all I've got to do
    is put my trust in Him
He has written the story book of my life
I walk by faith and not by sight
Gonna cast my cares aside,
    and give it all to Him

Faith in the unseen is hard
    when storms are blowing
But I know He promised me,
    the sun will shine again
He has prepared for me
    great things no eye has ever seen
I'm made for victory,
    so I stand firm believing

Season Twenty

It was a Saturday morning. Brian was at work and Devin had spent the night at a friend's house. I was having a personal time of praise and worship, while also working on a new song for church.

Ethan kept coming in and out of the room to see me. Then he would go back and watch TV or play a video game before returning once again.

"Mama, that's a pretty song," he said.

"Come over here and I will teach you the words, so you can sing it with me," I replied. He caught on quickly because he had been listening to me practice.

He sang the words: "Oh Holy God, I stay amazed; you are so much more than words could ever say. Oh Holy God, I pour out my praise, to the one who never ceases to amaze." (Words from the song "Stay Amazed" © by Gateway Worship 2010).

It was the most beautiful thing I had ever heard. This was my little boy who was not supposed to speak, let alone sing. Now he was singing words from the bottom of his heart.

I shut off the music and said, "Ethan, I want to talk about staying amazed. God has done something amazing in our life. We can never forget or take this miracle lightly."

He said, "Oh, I know, Mama! God healed me! He is the one who did it. I couldn't talk before, and now I talk all the time. And I know God healed me from eighteen food allergies."

I said, "That's right, Ethan. God loves you so much. We will always give God the glory for what has happened. Let's sing this song again and thank God together."

As we began to sing again, Ethan's beautiful blue eyes filled with tears. I lifted his hands up to the heavens and told him, "This is how we thank God for His great and mighty works." I felt the peace of God come in the room as we sang. Ethan started crying like I have never seen him cry. Clearly, he felt the presence of God as we stood there with our hands raised to heaven.

I pulled him into my arms and held him. As I held him, his little body shook; it was not out of fear but with a heart of thanks. He felt God; the presence of God had touched him. We both cried tears of joy and shared a true God moment.

For the first time, Ethan understood what God had done. He not only acknowledged his healing with his mouth, he felt it and expressed it with his heart.

As we sat there, I spoke into his life and his future. "Ethan, you have come so far—you have friends at school, friends at church, and you're the smartest one in your class. You are going to go to high school and then college, and even there you'll be the smartest one. You're going to graduate and then get married and have kids of your own. I can't wait to see all of the great things that you are going to do."

We may have come to the end of this book, but definitely not the end of the story. God said that He knows Ethan by name and He has a plan and a future for Him.

Is Ethan perfect? No. But what child is? Will he have bumps in the road? Probably, but God never promised us that this journey called life would be easy. Although, He did promise us, that He would never leave us, nor forsake us.

Brian, Devin, Ethan, and I know that God has brought us this far, and only He will continue to lead and guide us to the end. Only God knows what the future holds, and because of this, we know that everything's going to be alright.

IT'S GONNA
BE ALRIGHT

I dwell in the shelter of the most high
I rest in the shadow of the almighty
I say, you are my refuge
My fortress, my God
In whom I trust all my days

I will not fear the terror of night
I won't worry about the arrows
    that fly by day
I'm standing, when a thousand
    may fall at my side
Cause all the angels, will guide
    me in all of my ways

It's gonna be alright, it's gonna be ok
God is on my side, making a way
I'm covered with your wings
I'm living in your grace
Lord you're all I need
And I give you praise

If my God is for me, who can be against me
I will not fear, I will not be afraid

I won't worry, it's gonna be alright
I won't worry, it's gonna be ok

A BRAND NEW DAY

Through water and through fire
You have brought us through
Through the greatness of your power
We have seen your awesome works

Through battles, through struggles
We have overcome the world
In all that we've been through
We are held by You

Whoa, the Son is shining
It's a brand new Day
Whoa, all the clouds are gone
Old things have passed away
I give my heart, I give a thousand thanks
It's a brand new day

Through victory and through trial
I fix my eyes on You
Every minute, every mile
You grace has brought me through
This is it; I'm living, the day
    the Lord has made
And I will rejoice, I'll be glad in it

Whoa, the Son is shining
It's a brand new Day
Whoa, all the clouds are gone
Old things have passed away
I give my heart, I give a thousand thanks
It's a brand new day

Song Credits

I'm Yours—Gina Walden and David Archibeck © 2010

I Surrender—Gina Walden and Gabee Mora© 2008

My Daughter—Gina Walden © 2007

Rock of My Salvation—Gina Walden, Gabee
   Mora and Cameron Ruffin © 2008

Oh Most High—Gina Walden and
   David Archibeck © 2010

Be Still—Gina Walden and Cameron Ruffin © 2011

I've Got Joy—Gina Walden and
   Cameron Ruffin © 2011

I Will Run—Gina Walden, Elijah Young
   and Cameron Ruffin © 2011

Storybook—Gina Walden and Cameron Ruffin © 2011

It's Gonna Be Alright—Gina Walden © 2010

A Brand New Day—Gina Walden
   and Kathie Obeso © 2010

For booking information or to purchase
the music from "A Brand New Day," go to:

abrandnewday.org

facebook.com/ginawaldenmusic

youtube.com/ginawaldenmusic